AWAKENED

A 52-WEEK
PROGRESSIVE
CHRISTIAN DEVOTIONAL

CALEB J. LINES

chalice
PRESS

Print: 9780827201293

EPUB: 9780827201309

EPDF: 9780827201316

ChalicePress.com

Printed in the United States of America

This book is dedicated

to Progressive Christians,

especially those who have supported the work of

ProgressiveChristianity.org (The Center for Progressive Christianity);

to University Christian Church; and

to Shawnna, Kit, Rosie, Kim, and Linda Lines.

CONTENTS

INTRODUCTION

Faith is a journey, not a destination. The Bible is a traveling companion, not a road map. We are spiritual pilgrims, not religious hermits.

Religion is ultimately about giving us the tools to navigate our lives, not to provide a divine answer key. Many religious traditions speak about a spiritual awakening, in which we become more attuned to God's presence around us. This devotional is designed to do exactly that from a Progressive Christian perspective. Christian devotionals are rather odd. They are mostly written by and for evangelicals and contain theology that makes most Progressive Christians very uncomfortable. In some ways, it might seem as if a progressive devotional is a contradiction in terms. Progressive Christianity has tended to be highly intellectual and has often deemphasized the spiritual aspects of religion to the point that they might seem unimportant. That shouldn't be the case! At its heart, Progressive Christianity is about being open to new and ancient ideas and experiences that expand our faith. I hope this book will help you to deepen yours.

By becoming *awakened*, I mean both an inward and outward change. In Buddhism, experiencing an awakening is paramount. The word "awakening" is connected to the notion of enlightenment, and the very title "Buddha" means "the awakened one." Buddhists often talk about developing a Buddha nature, which in part means becoming awakened. We Christians ought to develop a Christ nature that involves a similar awakening: an inward change that leads to outward action.

In popular culture, the awakening toward outward action could be described as becoming "woke." That term has its origins with

Black Americans, who have been using it for decades. Originally, the phrase related to being aware of systemic racial injustice. But over the past few years, it has become synonymous with awareness about all sorts of justice issues: sexism, xenophobia, homophobia, transphobia, income inequality, and climate change, to name a few. In the wake of George Floyd's murder in 2020 and the Black Lives Matter protests that followed, those on the political and religious right began to use this word as a derogatory term against anyone who was pursuing social justice. In response to this derogatory use of "woke," I created and posted a meme. It featured a picture of a historically accurate Middle Eastern Jesus and said, "Jesus was woke: He was awakened to the needs of others and called out systems of oppression. Be like Jesus. Be woke."

Jesus was *awakened* to the needs of others—so much so that the Romans murdered him for his actions. Jesus proclaimed the Reign of God on Earth in stark contrast to the oppressive forces of Rome. The Reign of God is a radical vision for the future in which the realities of injustice with which God's people lived are flipped on their heads. In the Reign of God, people have plenty of food to eat, the world is permeated by love and justice instead of hatred and inequality, all are radically included, and, most importantly, we show our ultimate allegiance to God, not to the worldly powers and systems. It is this belief, this vision, that prompted the Romans to execute Jesus for insurrection. Jesus was all about becoming so awake to God's presence that we transform ourselves, the religious establishment, and political institutions.

On the cover of this book, there is a picture of one sheep looking up from the flock while all the others are looking down. I love this image. One sheep has awakened and can see what others cannot. The Bible often describes God as a shepherd, and if we are guided or shepherded to anything through the teachings of Jesus it ought to be an awakening to our own spiritual life, an awakening that then prompts us to create a more just and peaceful world. The sheep has awakened. So shall we.

Guiding Values

We Progressive Christians are a big tent group, by which I mean that we fling our arms wide open, we acknowledge that there is no one right way to be a Christian or to interpret scripture. Nonetheless, there are certain values which most Progressive Christians share. At ProgressiveChristianity.org, we have developed Five Core Values that distinguish Progressive Christians from others. Those values guide this devotional and appear below.

By calling ourselves Progressive Christians, we mean that we are Christians who...

1. Believe that following the way and teachings of Jesus can lead to experiencing sacredness, wholeness, and unity of all life, even as we recognize that the Spirit moves in beneficial ways in many faith traditions;

2. Seek community that is inclusive of all people, honoring differences in theological perspective, age, race, sexual orientation, gender identity/expression, class, and ability;

3. Strive for peace and justice among all people, knowing that behaving with compassion and selfless love towards one another is the fullest expression of what we believe;

4. Embrace the insights of contemporary science and strive to protect the Earth, and ensure its integrity and sustainability; and

5. Commit to a path of life-long learning, believing there is more value in questioning than in absolutes.[1]

How to Use This Devotional

Awakened is a fifty-two-week companion on your spiritual journey. You need not confess any creed or belong to a specific tradition to use it. If you consider yourself to be spiritual but not religious, this may be your book! The book can be read individually, in small groups, or as an entire faith community. Because it is not year-specific, it can be used multiple times. It is meant to guide you through the year, deepen your spirituality, and introduce

---

[1] ProgressiveChristianity.org, "The Core Values of Progressive Christianity," 2022, https://progressivechristianity.org/the-core-values-of-progressive-christianity/.

you to Progressive Christian principles. It is structured around thirteen Progressive Christian themes and there are four weeks of devotions per theme. The themes are separate, so you can read them at any point in the year, and in any order—though below I suggest you read them in a particular order, and why:

1. Renewal—January, New Year
2. Diversity—February, Black History Month
3. Biblical Women—March, Women's History Month
4. Eco-Spirituality—April, Earth Day/Arbor Day
5. Mental Health—May, Mental Health Awareness Month
6. LGBTQ+ Affirmation—June, Pride Month
7. Reign of God—July, US Independence Day
8. Questioning—Late Summer/Early Fall
9. Faith in Science—Late Summer/Early Fall
10. Embracing Change—Fall
11. Rethinking Beliefs—Fall
12. Gratitude—November, Thanksgiving
13. Christmas—December, Christmas

Each devotion contains the following:

1. A Centering Scripture. This frames the week's devotion.
2. A Reflection. I connect the theme for the day with a spiritual reflection and with your life and the world.
3. Discussion Questions. If you are reading this book in a group, these questions can facilitate discussion. If you are reading this book on your own, thinking through these questions can enhance your awakening. You might want to write your responses in a journal or on a note app.
4. A Spiritual Practice. Awakening does not typically happen without intentional effort and preparation.

These spiritual practices are designed to help with your journey toward awakening by offering a diverse set of practices.

5. A video to watch mid-week. Each devotion has a companion video, in which I discuss themes in greater detail and lead you through that week's spiritual practice. If you read the devotion on Sunday and watch the video on Wednesday, you'll have two points during the week at which you are specifically focusing on your spiritual journey. Access the videos by scanning the QR Code on the cover of this book with your phone.

A Word about Bible Translations

There are many Bible translations, but they're not all created equal! While all translations require interpretive decisions, some versions of the Bible contain translations that promote a certain theological agenda. Others, like *The Message*, are more of a paraphrase and interpretation than an actual translation. To understand the original intent of texts most clearly, translations that strive to translate directly are preferable. For this devotional, I've chosen the New Revised Standard Version Updated Edition. This version includes some important updates to the New Revised Standard Version that help with clarity and inclusive language. However, there are some instances in which I've used the New Revised Standard Version because of its familiar wording. I have also used *The Inclusive Bible* on a couple of occasions to avoid the preponderance of masculine language for God when it's not necessary to understand the scripture. If you choose to read the weekly scripture in your Bible (all three translations are available online!), it might be helpful to use the same version as in the devotional.

Explanation of Terminology

Jesus' primary focus was creating the Reign of God on Earth. Because it was so important to him, several of these weekly devotions address those teachings. In the New Testament, we read about the *Basileia* of God, which is often translated as "Kingdom." However, "Kingdom" is masculine language that infers that God is the "King" and that we are God's subjects, which doesn't truly represent the notion that Jesus describes. One popular alternative translation is "Kindom," which focuses on relationality (that we are all "kin") but doesn't carry a political dimension. Another is "Realm," which is similar in denotation to Kingdom, but often has a connotation in modern usage of something otherworldly. I have chosen "Reign" because it connotes a political element without setting God up as a "King" and us as God's subjects. Instead, it highlights loyalty to Jesus' alternative vision of the future, a future in which we no longer have systems of human domination, but we welcome God's reign in the world—God's rule over our hearts with peace, love, and justice.

RENEWAL

Week 1– Renewal: Letting Go

....

*So do not worry about tomorrow, for tomorrow will bring
worries of its own. Today's trouble is enough for today.
(Matthew 6:34)[1]*

Life is filled with worry. It sounds nice when Jesus urges us
not to worry, yet we know that anxiety and depression cannot
simply be dismissed by saying, "Don't worry about it, it's in God's
hands!" Further, assuming that God is in full control of our lives
is bad theology and is easily disproved. If God did control our
lives, this world would be in much better shape! Luckily, I don't
think Jesus is telling us to "let go and let God." Jesus gives this
instruction about worry during the Sermon on the Mount, which
includes some of his most powerful ethical teachings. He has
just finished instructing his listeners on how to pray and how to
avoid materialism. His instructions are not about avoiding worry
altogether, but rather about worrying about the right kinds of
things, mainly those things we can control in the here and now,
and letting go of things we can't control.

Jesus' instruction about worry is true not only of the future but
also of the past. Many people live with a sense of continual regret
about what happened in the past and what could have been. Yet,
our memories are figments of our imagination. We remember
what happened only through our perspective filtered through
time. Sometimes, we look back with rose-colored glasses when
recalling a time that truly wasn't as great as we remember. Or we
might look back and think about how awful a period was, forgetting
how we were blessed along the way. Centering ourselves in this
moment is a helpful exercise, even for those of us who live with
anxiety that is beyond our control, because it can help to keep our
minds from racing.

One of the most powerful teachings we can learn from our
Buddhist siblings is that our attachment to things and ideas is
one of the primary causes of suffering in our lives. Frequently, we
become attached to a certain expectation about how circumstances

---

[1] All quotations will be from the New Revised Standard Version
Updated Edition unless otherwise noted.

are supposed to go. If other people or our lives don't match our expectations, we suffer. It's natural to have hopes and dreams, but let's remember that the universe is under no obligation to live up to our expectations!

Many times, when we worry about the future, we envision thousands of possibilities of what *could* happen...typically the worst possible scenarios. Of course, 99.9 percent of those things will not and do not happen, and we have caused ourselves suffering for no reason. Simply put, *this very moment* is the only one that we have. The past is gone. The future is not guaranteed. Let's make the most of the moment that we have! We can use this moment to take stock of what is important in our lives and to focus on those areas that give us life. We can also use this grounding to avoid escapist theology. Many Christians are so concerned with the future (i.e., an afterlife) that they avoid looking at the present to see what work needs to be done now. The worries of today involve confronting the injustices that are before us and taking them on concretely in the here and now. May it be so. Amen.

QUESTIONS

- By what elements of your past are you being held back? What would it feel like to let them go?

- Which aspects of your past have concretely made you who you are? Which ones specifically define you?

- What is weighing on your heart about the future? Is it something that you can control?

- What are the most pressing concerns in your life at this moment?

- What are the most pressing needs of your community and of the world around you?

Spiritual Practice

Throughout our reflections on renewal, we will try a simple breathing meditation, with a few variations. To begin, find a comfortable position in a chair. Place your feet flat on the floor and feel the earth beneath you. Place your hands in a folded position on your lap. Close your eyes and try to clear your head as you focus on your breath. If thoughts come into your head, acknowledge them, and strive to let them go by concentrating solely on your breath. It may help to focus on a word or phrase. As you breathe in, try thinking "This moment..." and as you breathe out, try thinking "is all I'm guaranteed." If it's your first time meditating, set a timer for five minutes. After you've completed your meditation, slowly open your eyes. How do you feel?

Video Reflection

Don't forget to scan the QR Code on the cover of this book for more on this topic and a mid-week spiritual practice.

Week 2 - Renewal: Embracing a New Season

For everything there is a season, and a time for every matter under heaven: a time to be born, and a time to die; a time to plant, and a time to pluck up what is planted; a time to kill, and a time to heal; a time to break down, and a time to build up; a time to weep, and a time to laugh; a time to mourn, and a time to dance...[God] has made everything suitable for its time; moreover [God] has put a sense of past and future into their minds, yet they cannot find out what God has done from the beginning to the end. I know that there is nothing better for them than to be happy and enjoy themselves as long as they live; moreover, it is God's gift that all should eat and drink and take pleasure in all their toil. (Ecclesiastes 3:1-4, 11-13)

We humans are naturally conditioned to expect changes at certain times. Perhaps this is why so many people want to start fresh at the beginning of the year. Qoheleth, the teacher in Ecclesiastes, has a different perspective about the world than many of the other authors in the Bible: human beings aren't inherently evil, life is not about suffering, and adhering to a proper belief system does not mark us as special. Instead, we should recognize that life is filled with different seasons, good and bad. The bad times aren't punishment from God, just as the good times aren't a reward. Rather, the cycles of our lives are simply a natural part of living. As such, one of the best ways to survive this life is to enjoy the good times when they're here and to try to endure the tough times by finding glimpses of joy amid despair.

Qoheleth is on to something here! Many Christians believe in some form of predestination, whether they want to admit it or not. They believe that God has a plan for their lives and that whatever trials and tribulations they endure are a part of God's greater plan. I don't see the world like that, and I don't think that Qoheleth did either. Suffering is just a natural part of life, just as joy is a natural part of life. God does not control our lives but rather has promised to be present with us at all times and through all things. God will never abandon us. Isn't the promise of God's unconditional love through all things that we do and endure more powerful than believing that God is controlling the minutia of our lives?

I've been heavily influenced by the teachings of Taoism. In Taoism, there is an understanding that the Tao (or "the way"[2]) permeates all our lives. It is a force that connects all living things and, in doing so, our actions affect other living things. The Tao doesn't control our lives, but rather is like the current of a stream. If we are in tune with it, the current will carry us, but if we fight against it, the journey will be much more difficult.

What if we were to view God similarly? God does not control our lives but rather is subtly nudging us toward love and compassion. If we go in the direction of the nudges, it is like following the current toward the future that Jesus called the Reign of God. If we fight against the nudges, it makes our lives and the world more difficult. Perhaps through the course of this week you can strive to be more open to the opportunities that the universe is setting before you. Strive to be open to opportunities for kindness, compassion, listening, and generosity. Perhaps something as simple as being present to a friend in need. May it be so. Amen.

QUESTIONS

- Where do you see the current trajectory of your life leading?
- When have you felt a current in life pushing you towards something new?
- What would it be like to envision God as a force rather than a being?
- Who are the people in your life who help you to connect more fully with God and think about your life in helpful ways?

---

[2] "The Way" is also the earliest name for the Jesus Movement that eventually became Christianity. During the early days following Jesus' crucifixion when most of his followers were still Jewish, saying that you were a follower of "The Way" was a way to differentiate yourself from others.

Spiritual Practice

Let's expand on the breathing meditation from last week. Find a comfortable position in a chair. Place your feet flat on the floor and feel the earth beneath you. Place your hands in a folded position on your lap. Close your eyes and try to clear your head by focusing on your breath. As you're breathing, strive to be open to God's presence. Can you feel any currents moving in your life? What is giving you great joy? Spend some time thinking quietly about what is giving you joy at this moment and to be grateful for it. If your last meditation was short, try to allow yourself some more time. Perhaps go from five minutes to ten minutes or some other incremental increase. After you've completed your meditation, slowly open your eyes. Focusing on the joy in our lives is always a good practice but can be an especially helpful tool during the rough seasons of our lives.

Video Reflection

Don't forget to scan the QR Code on the cover of this book for more on this topic and a mid-week spiritual practice.

Week 3 - Renewal: Rebirth

....

Do not remember the former things or consider the things of old. I am about to do a new thing; now it springs forth, do you not perceive it? I will make a way in the wilderness and rivers in the desert. (Isaiah 43:18-19).

Each day is an opportunity for growth and renewal. It's important to recognize that life is filled with deaths and rebirths. We might try something for a while and it may be a good fit for a time, but just because we've decided to try something doesn't mean that we must be stuck with it! Perhaps you've seen the meme that says, "Don't cling to a mistake just because you've spent a lot of time making it!" It's not that our lives are measured in successes and failures, as our culture tells us that they are. Perhaps, instead, they're a series of instances in which we've done the best we could and made the best decisions we were able at the time. Sometimes those are decisions that remain helpful, and sometimes they are decisions that we wouldn't make again based on the changes in our life experience. It's all well to permit ourselves to try new things continually, and to allow them to stick if they are helpful and to die if they're not. This can be as simple as engaging in a new exercise routine or as difficult as recognizing that a relationship needs to end because it is no longer healthy.

In Isaiah, the ancient Israelites live in Babylonian captivity and life is extremely difficult. The words in today's centering scripture are intended as a message of hope so those who are exiled will recognize that there will be something else beyond the current situation. The time of suffering will end, and a new time of rejoicing will begin. Endings and beginnings are a constant in our lives, yet for rebirth to happen, death must occur. One of the intriguing teachings from Eastern religious traditions such as Hinduism and Buddhism is that life is a continual cycle: birth, life, death, and rebirth. While I don't subscribe to the notion that our soul cycles through various lives, science has taught us that this rebirth cycle is factual in some respects. The atoms that make up our body are released when we die and become something else entirely. In fact, all the atoms in us and around us were once a part of collapsing stars. Carl Sagan spoke the truth when he said, "The nitrogen in our DNA, the calcium in our teeth, the iron in our blood, the carbon in our apple pies, were made in the interiors of collapsing stars. We are made of star stuff."[3]

Our connection to each other and the universe is very real. We share the same atoms! Things that have been a part of our lives up to this point will remain with us, for better or worse. Yet, if something is no longer helpful, it's okay to let it die figuratively because it is only through death that a rebirth is possible. Hold on to what is helpful. Permit yourself to let go of what is not.

May it be so. Amen

QUESTIONS

- When have you let go of something that was no longer helpful?

- When have you let go of previous religious beliefs and embraced new ones?

- When have you held on to prejudices about others that you later revised based on growth?

- What are you holding on to that is no longer helpful? What would it feel like to let it go?

- What would it feel like to let go of the notion of failures and successes in your life and to be more forgiving of yourself?

Spiritual Practice

This week, we'll continue to expand on the breathing meditations of the last two weeks. Find a comfortable position in a chair. Place your feet flat on the floor and feel the earth beneath you. Place your hands in a folded position on your lap. Close your eyes and try to clear your head, as you focus on your breath. After a time of centering, think about something of which it would be helpful to let go. If your last meditation was short, try to give yourself a bit more time this time. Perhaps go from ten to fifteen minutes,

[3] Carl Sagan, *Cosmos* (New York: Ballantine Books, 1980), 190.

or some other incremental increase. After you've completed your meditation, slowly open your eyes.

Video Reflection

Don't forget to scan the QR Code on the cover of this book for more on this topic and a mid-week spiritual practice.

Week 4 – Renewal: New Creation

....

So if anyone is in Christ, there is a new creation: everything
old has passed away; look, new things have come into being!
(2 Corinthians 5:17)

I grew up in a tradition that practices believer's baptism by full
immersion. Around the time I was in middle school, I started to
feel that I wanted to dedicate my life to following the teachings of
Jesus. My congregation never talked about a moment of salvation,
and I didn't think about baptism in terms of "getting saved,"
even though that salvation narrative pervades our culture. Still,
I expected something to be different on the other side of the
baptismal waters. I was surprised to find that life was pretty much
the same on the other side. Later I realized that's because baptism
is just the beginning of the journey to follow Jesus. Baptism was the
beginning of Jesus' journey, too. Some scholars suggest that Jesus
was a follower of John the Baptist and that he took up John's mantle
once John was arrested by the Romans. This explanation helps us
to make sense of why the biblical narrative accounts for so little of
Jesus' life. He wasn't doing ministry until he was inspired to begin
a new path. In fact, there was a whole strain of early Christians
who believed that Jesus was just an ordinary human being until
God adopted him at baptism. Appropriately enough, they were
known as Jewish-Christian Adoptionists.[4]

Sometimes we experience significant events in our lives that
radically change our trajectory. More often, though, change
happens gradually. Living into our sense of being a new creation
is something that is ongoing and changes with age, social location,
physical location, and experience. Being a follower of Jesus also
looks different depending on our life experience, and it should
never become stagnant. One of the most significant heresies of
American Christianity is the notion of a single salvific experience
that acts as a "Get out of Hell Free" card for your whole life. The

---

[4] Bart Ehrman, *The New Testament: A Historical Introduction to the*
Early Christian Writings, 3rd ed. (Oxford: Oxford University Press, 2004),
3.

notion of Hell is bad, unbiblical theology anyway,[5] but the idea that following Jesus requires nothing more from us than a mere confession of salvation misses the entire point of his ministry.

Jesus' ministry was all about loving others and caring for those on the margins. If we want to put the gospel into a single word, it's "love." It's as easy as that—and as hard as that. Perhaps it seems trite to say that the gospel is love or that God is love. Yet loving is not easy. It's hard to love our enemies. Sometimes it's hard to love the people we love! Becoming a new creation in Christ involves a lot of practice, a lot of missteps, and a continual commitment to keep trying anyway. May it be so.

QUESTIONS

- What led you to commit yourself to following Jesus' teachings?
- Have your beliefs changed over time?
- What would it feel like to allow yourself the freedom to have different beliefs ten years from now?
- When could you have done better at following Jesus' teachings?
- When did you surprise yourself by being more loving because of your faith?

Spiritual Practice

This week, we'll conclude our weekly breathing meditation exercises. Find a comfortable position in a chair. Place your feet on the floor and feel the earth beneath you. Place your hands in a folded position on your lap. Close your eyes and try to clear your head, as you focus on your breath. Think of a time when you clearly felt God's presence. This time try a focus phrase: as you're breathing in, say to yourself, "Breath of God" and as you exhale, "Peace of Christ." If your last meditation was short, try to give yourself a bit more time. Perhaps go from fifteen to twenty minutes

---

[5] When Jesus used the word *Gehenna*, which is often translated as "Hell," he was referring to a literal valley where children had been sacrificed to pagan gods.

or some other incremental increase. After you've completed your meditation, slowly open your eyes.

Video Reflection

Don't forget to scan the QR Code on the cover of this book for more on this topic and a mid-week spiritual practice.

DIVERSITY

Week 5 - Diversity: Embracing Our Differences

For just as the body is one and has many members, and all the members of the body, though many, are one body, so it is with Christ. For in the one Spirit we were all baptized into one body—Jews or Greeks, slaves or free—and we were all made to drink of one Spirit. Indeed, the body does not consist of one member but of many. (1 Corinthians 12:12-14)

I sometimes struggle with Paul. Pieces of his letters are harsh and offensive, while other portions are so beautiful that they bring tears to my eyes. Perhaps because Paul was so prolific, we get to see him as more whole and real than other biblical writers. Yet despite my complicated relationship with Paul, it's clear to me that Paul understood the concept of community. He recognized that community doesn't truly work unless we're all in it together. For many years, White America had a narrative that all people are basically the same and so we should try to ignore our differences and focus on our commonalities: that we should be "colorblind." While there may have been good intentions behind this focus— though, let's be honest, it was probably more about trying to make white people feel comfortable and less about addressing any inequality—it led to harmful ways of dealing with the world. If we don't acknowledge our differences, how can we be truly awakened to the needs of others, attuned to their needs?

Paul thought that divisions should disappear within the community of Jesus-followers, but that didn't mean that he thought that every difference would literally disappear. From his letters, it's clear that there was plenty that divided the early community. In this week's passage from 1 Corinthians, he makes it clear that people are, in fact, different, and that the only way the body of Christ can function is if we embrace those distinctions as gifts from God. As he says in v. 17, "If the whole body were an eye, where would the hearing be? If the whole body were hearing, where would the sense of smell be?" Yes, Paul wants us to embrace our gifts, but it's more than that: it's about being who we are authentically, while also embracing others as they are. Paul recognizes that if we are all, in fact, created in God's image, then living as an authentic reflection of God honors God.

After police officers murdered George Floyd in 2020, much of the American cultural narrative (let's be honest: the *white* cultural narrative) about racial progress was dismantled as the country looked with fresh eyes at what communities of color had always known: the United States continues to have deep-seated structural and personal racism, one that is contrary to the Christian Gospel. The gospel calls us to see each person as a child of God with inherent worth and dignity. The gospel calls us to look for systems of injustice and oppression and to tear them down. This begins by both looking at our places of bias—because we *all* have them—and recognizing that US systems are built to favor those who are white, male, property owners. One of the most courageous acts of faith in which we can engage is to become aware of how we see others and to reframe our minds to see every individual person as a reflection of God...recognizing that diversity is beautiful and teaches us more about God in our lives and our world. May it be so.

QUESTIONS

- When did you become aware of a bias within yourself?
- How have you experienced oppression in your own life?
- When have you seen others being marginalized and found a way to lend your voice to support them?
- When have you fallen into the trap of claiming to be "colorblind" or that "we're all essentially the same?"
- What would it feel like to try throughout the week to strive to see each person you encounter as a child of God?

Spiritual Practice

Over the years, I've come to believe that some of the most powerful prayers come in the form of conversations. Perhaps because I'm such an extrovert by nature, conversations are a way for me to process my thoughts and experiences, while also hearing perspectives from others.

Over the course of the next few weeks, our spiritual practice will be attempting to engage in Holy Conversations. This week, try to think of someone in your life who's had different life experiences than you have had. If you're able to do so, create space to speak with them about their life and experience. It doesn't need to be an interview or anything formal: just have coffee and a conversation. Take note of the places of convergence and divergence with your own story. At the end of your conversation think about what you learned about God from the other person.

Video Reflection

Don't forget to scan the QR Code on the cover of this book for more on this topic and a mid-week spiritual practice.

Week 6 – Diversity: Confronting our own Biases

[The Lawyer] answered [Jesus], "You shall love the Lord your God with all your heart and with all your soul and with all your strength and with all your mind and your neighbor as yourself." And he said to him, "You have given the right answer; do this, and you will live." But wanting to vindicate himself, he asked Jesus, "And who is my neighbor?" (Luke 10:27-29)

We all know what happens next: Jesus tells the story of the Good Samaritan to teach us that absolutely everyone is our neighbor. Except many of us miss the powerful point about overcoming xenophobia that is inherent in this parable. A Judean is beaten and left for dead on the side of the road. This made him ritually impure and thus anyone who encountered him would have become impure as well. A priest and a Levite both pass by the injured man, but cross to the other side of the road. Why? Because if they had contact with the man, they would have become impure and wouldn't have been able to go to the Temple to fulfill their religious obligations. We might expect religious leaders to be the first to go out of their way to help someone in need, but we also know that religious hypocrisy is something that permeates all times, cultures, and spaces; these religious leaders go on and offer no help. It is the Samaritan who stops and helps.

Samaritans were once a part of the same culture, but during Jesus' time, they were foreigners. "Foreigner" is not quite strong enough a word, though. Despite their common heritage, Judeans looked down on the Samaritans, and saw them as a sort-of "half-breed." The Samaritan isn't just a kind stranger who went out of his way to help someone he didn't know; he was one of the least likely heroes that Jesus' followers would have been able to imagine. Hearing this story wouldn't simply have presented the Judean audience with a passing challenge to be more aware of the needs of others: the seven-verse parable throws all their cultural biases thrown at them! Moreover, our hero didn't merely pick up the stranger, dust him off, and send him on his way. No: he bandaged the injured Judean, placed him on his own animal while he walked, took him to an inn, paid for his care, and told the innkeeper that he would pay any additional costs necessary for the stranger's recovery. Talk about a hero!

Reflecting on how we can help those in need is certainly a good lesson to take from this parable, but it overlooks its most central points: that God works with and through those we least expect, and that God does not subscribe to our prejudices. Imagine yourself by the side of the road in desperate need of help. Imagine a pastor and a church leader crossing to the other side of the road and leaving you for dead. Now imagine someone you least expect stopping to help: an undocumented person who has just crossed the border, someone from a different religious group whom we may not completely understand, or maybe even someone from a different political party with whom we strongly disagree. Now imagine the situation being reversed and you seeing someone radically different from you in need of your care.

One of the most powerful things about Jesus' teachings is that he is always asking us to expand our field of compassion. He always asks us to love more deeply and to welcome more radically. That's a message that goes far beyond Galilee two thousand years ago. Who is your neighbor today? Everyone, but especially those who you least expect. May it be so. Amen.

QUESTIONS

- What kind of person would you least expect to help you?

- What kind of person would you have the hardest time helping?

- Whom have you seen in a new way after spending time with them?

- What might it feel like to be less defined by borders, real and societal?

- How can we overcome cultural, theological, or political differences?

Spiritual Practice

This week, we will continue our Holy Conversation practice. Think of someone whom you find difficult to be around. Perhaps through this week's reflection and questions you identified a group of people about whom you have some assumptions. Is it possible to get to know someone from one of those groups? Someone from a different religious tradition? Someone from a different country of origin? Someone whose culture is different from yours? Perhaps merely pushing yourself to make small talk with someone is a good first step. As you engage with them, think to yourself, "We are both children of God, created in God's image." Afterward, reflect on what you learned about God from your conversation.

Video Reflection

Don't forget to scan the QR Code on the cover of this book for more on this topic and a mid-week spiritual practice.

Week 7 – Diversity: Confronting Structures

··

*Perhaps this is the reason [Onesimus] was separated from you
for a while, so that you might have him back forever, no longer
as a slave but more than a slave, a beloved brother—especially
to me but how much more to you, both in the flesh and in the
Lord. So if you consider me your partner, welcome him as you
would welcome me. (Philemon 1:15–17)*

Christians must deal with the reality that the Bible is not inherently
good or bad, but rather a tool that we can use to propel us to either
greater love or unconscionable evil. We need look no further than
the historical fact that Christians in the United States used the
Bible to justify slavery and that some of the most fervent white
nationalists today consider themselves to be Christians. Slavery
was a reality in the socio-historical context of the Bible, but it
was not merely the racially motivated slavery that was present in
the United States. There were different types of slavery in Jesus'
day including enslavement of foreigners, of prisoners of war,
of those who were highly indebted, sexual slavery, and so forth.
Jesus is shockingly silent on the issue of slavery, and his teachings
regarding it seem to acknowledge it as a cultural reality without
proclaiming the type of liberation that we'd expect to see. Jesus
heals a centurion's slave,[1] but only after the centurion makes the
case that the slave is worthy of being healed. Jesus tells parables
that include slaves, but he doesn't comment on their status (i.e.,
the story of the Prodigal Son[2] in which the father asks his slaves
to prepare a feast on his son's return)[3]. Jesus also speaks about
spiritual slavery, for instance when he says, "No one can serve
two masters, for a slave will either hate the one and love the other
or be devoted to the one and despise the other. You cannot serve
God and wealth."[4] In the Gospel of Matthew, Jesus does say that

---

[1] Luke 7:1–10.

[2] Luke 15:11–32.

[3] Other stories like this include the Parable of the Talents (Mt.
25:14–30, Lk. 19:11–27), the Parable of the Unforgiving Servant (Mt.
18:21–35), the Parable of the Bad Tenants (Mt. 21:33–46, Mk. 12:1–12,
Lk. 20:9–19).

[4] Matthew 6:24.

he gives rest to those who labor,[5] but he does not mention slaves specifically.

Paul seems to believe that, at least in theory, enslavement shouldn't exist in the Christian community,[6] but Paul also believed that the world was going to end within his lifetime and that everyone should stay within the boundaries of their current social roles.[7] In this week's centering scripture, Paul is writing a letter to Philemon, who is the leader of the church in Colossae. While in prison, Paul encountered Onesimus who was enslaved to Philemon but has escaped. After hearing the gospel from Paul, Onesimus converted to Christianity and is now returning to Philemon. In the letter, Paul asks Philemon to regard the returning Onesimus not as a slave, but as a sibling in Christ. He doesn't seem to be advocating the upheaval of the slavery system, however. Instead, since Onesimus had already escaped and had then converted to Christianity, where there is to be "neither slave nor free," he asks Philemon to release Onesimus from slavery.

Reading the stories of slavery in the New Testament reminds us that the Bible and the people in it are products of their time. Wanting the Bible to speak to our current social realities often leaves us desiring much more than the text will ever be able to deliver. This is why it's important to understand the socio-historical context and to recognize why the Bible covers some subjects and not others. Throughout the gospels, Jesus gives us the criterion of love. He does this most clearly in the synoptic gospels by affirming that the greatest two commandments are to love God and neighbor. That means that our theological interpretation must always pass the criterion of love or else it is not a valid theological position. Could people use the Bible to justify racism generally, or slavery specifically? Yes, and plenty of Christians have done exactly that. However, using the Bible in a way that maligns or actively oppresses people does not pass the criterion of love and thus is appalling theology. This is also why continuing to write words about God or theology remains important. The United Church of Christ's slogan, "God is Still Speaking" means that we should be open to ongoing

---

[5] Matthew 11:28.

[6] Take his argument that in Christ there is neither slave nor free in 1 Corinthians 12:13, for instance.

[7] Cf. 1 Corinthian 7:29-31.

theological conversation. Even though ecumenical councils voted to close the biblical canon, that doesn't mean that we should close our minds to new thoughts about God. The Bible leaves much to be desired in condemning some of the most horrific institutions ever invented by humanity, which means that it is up to modern Christians to condemn the root causes. While the official institution of slavery no longer exists, new iterations are palpable in the US. One such example is the prison system, which disproportionately incarcerates (enslaves) people of color, especially young black men. We must continue to be vocal in addressing the causes of systemic and personal racism. May it be so. Amen.

QUESTIONS

- What do you think about using the criterion of love as a litmus test for theology?
- Can you think of institutions that are modern forms of slavery?
- Do you think that God continues to reveal the truth, or was it revealed perfectly in the Bible?
- What other biblical texts promote problematic moral stances?
- What are other matters about which you find the Bible oddly silent?

Spiritual Practice

This week, we will continue our Holy Conversation practice. Try to speak to someone who has had a different life experience than you. For example, do you know someone who has been or is incarcerated? What is or was their experience like? Think about what you learned about God from your conversation.

Video Reflection

Don't forget to scan the QR Code on the cover of this book for more on this topic and a mid-week spiritual practice.

Week 8 – Diversity: Liberation

....

Then the Lord said to Moses, "Go to Pharaoh, and say to him,
'Thus says the Lord, the God of the Hebrews: Let my people go,
so that they may serve me.'" (Exodus 9:1)

You're probably familiar with the general narrative of the Exodus story, but let me recap the highlights, just in case. It begins with Joseph being sold into slavery and through a series of events he becomes an advisor to the Pharoah in Egypt. Joseph advises the Pharaoh to store up grain in anticipation of a drought, and when that drought arrives Joseph's people come to Egypt in search of food. Generations go by and the Egyptians forget how the Israelite Joseph helped them, and they enslave the ancient Israelites. God chooses Moses to liberate God's people, and after Moses stands up to the pharaoh, there follow a series of plagues, a harrowing escape, and forty years of wilderness-wandering before the ancient Israelites are free. From this story, Liberation theologians proclaim a God who desires all people to be free. Yet, human beings oppress each other time and again. We are all, every one of us, children of God who are created in the divine image and who have inherent worth and dignity. Systems that perpetuate oppression and marginalization are sinful, and we all have a moral obligation to dismantle them. Narratively, the Exodus story is one that we need to tell, because Moses acts as a prophetic witness for God, demanding that those who are enslaved be released. The Pharaoh resists, as people in power always do when others demand liberation from them, and God intervenes to help God's people. It's a powerful story, and re-telling it is a way of keeping front of mind God's desire for liberation.

Of course, while narratively powerful, the Exodus story is not historically factual. There was no great, one-time liberation, but the general threads of the story are historical. There may not have been a Joseph who was sold into slavery and who ascended the Egyptian ranks. However, archaeological evidence amply supports that people from Canaan moved to Egypt's fertile Nile Valley during times of drought.[8] Whether these people were ever

---

[8] Israel Finkelstein and Neil Asher Silberman, *The Bible Unearthed: Archaeology's New Vision of Ancient Israel and the Origin of Its Sacred Texts* (New York: Free Press, 2001), 52.

enslaved or led by a figure named Moses is a hotly debated topic amongst Hebrew Bible scholars and is ultimately impossible to know. Regardless of Moses' historicity, it is highly unlikely that there was ever a mass exodus of enslaved people from Egypt to Canaan, however, because the Egyptians kept a tight border and excellent records; they recorded no such mass exodus.[9] However, there is archeological evidence of Egyptian artifacts appearing in the northern kingdom of Israel over several centuries indicating that there may have been several smaller exoduses instead of one large exodus. Hebrew Bible scholar John J. Collins puts it like this: "Some scholars now suppose that the biblical account may have 'telescoped' several small exoduses, which took place over centuries, into one dramatic narrative."[10]

Some readers may find this disappointing, but I think it's hopeful. If we really believe that God is at work in the world—and I do— then don't we want to know what actually happened? Looking at history gets rid of the problematic theology that results from a literal reading of the text. In the story, God imposes plagues— including infanticide—against all Egyptians, even those who had no control over what those in power were doing. In the story, God kills the entire Egyptian army with water as the ancient Israelites make their escape. In the story, after forty years of wandering, the ancient Israelites finally reach the Promised Land and discover that there are already people living there; God has the ancient Israelites slaughter those pesky Canaanite inhabitants. Historically, that's not what happened. People made it to freedom little by little, generation by generation, hopeful traveler by hopeful traveler, until everyone was free. It strikes me that God often liberates in that way: one person at a time, one moment at a time, one hard-fought fight after another. People shouldn't have to wait, and that's why the grand narrative is important. But the real history reminds us never to give up, but rather to keep going, even when liberation seems impossible. May it be so. Amen.

---

[9] John J. Collins, *Introduction to the Hebrew Bible* (Minneapolis: Fortress Press, 2004), 108.
[10] Collins, *Introduction to the Hebrew Bible*, 109.

QUESTIONS

- Does the historical understanding of the exodus change the way you think about it?

- What would it mean to embrace the truth of grand narrative, while also learning historical facts?

- What are some examples of small liberations that you have seen in your own life, or our broader narrative?

- What are some ways that we can help hasten the liberation of oppressed peoples?

- Who is a modern Moses leading people to freedom?

Spiritual Practice

This week, we will continue our Holy Conversation practice. Think of someone you admire who's doing work to help others. Create space to have a conversation with them and find out more about their work. What did you learn about God from your conversation?

Video Reflection

Don't forget to scan the QR Code on the cover of this book for more on this topic and a mid-week spiritual practice.

BIBLICAL WOMEN

Week 9 – Biblical Women: Teaching Jesus a Lesson

....

> *Now the woman was a gentile, of Syrophoenician origin. She*
> *begged him to cast the demon out of her daughter. He said to*
> *her, "Let the children be fed first, for it is not fair to take the*
> *children's food and throw it to the dogs." But she answered him,*
> *"Sir, even the dogs under the table eat the children's crumbs."*
> *Then he said to her, "For saying that, you may go—the demon*
> *has left your daughter." And when she went home, she found*
> *the child lying on the bed and the demon gone. (Mark 7:26-30)*

The story of the Syrophoenician woman[1] is one of my favorites in the Bible because there's nothing else quite like it. Jesus' ministry has been tiring, and he's ready to rest. We discover that he has entered a house and doesn't want anyone to know he's there. Just as he's settling in, this woman shows up, desperate and begging for Jesus to heal her daughter. The Syrophoenician woman was marginalized in multiple ways, she isn't even given a name in the story. She was a woman so she had limited rights in the ancient world. On top of that, she knelt at Jesus' feet, which was scandalous because people were not supposed to touch the feet of people of the opposite sex.[2] She was a foreigner, and simply for that reason, people in Jesus' land would have looked down on her. Simply put, it's surprising that the Syrophoenician woman approaches Jesus at all. She has no reason other than his reputation to expect him to help her.

She approaches Jesus to ask for help. What is Jesus' response? It's not what we expect. Even though Jesus has spent his whole ministry advocating for people on the margins, he says, "Let the children be fed first, for it is not fair to take the children's food and throw it to the dogs." Jesus is essentially saying, "Lady, I need to take care of my people first. How can I take care of you foreigners (he literally calls her a dog) when I've got to serve my own people?" Some scholars try to twist Jesus' words and say that he uses the diminutive form of "dog", so it's not so bad, he's calling

---

[1] A Canaanite woman in Matthew's version, Mt. 15:21-28.

[2] Think about the woman who washes Jesus' feet with her hair or the biblical euphemism for sex, "uncovering feet."

her a puppy. Some try to say that it was a compliment to compare someone to a dog. Some say that Jesus was simply trying to teach her a lesson in patience and persistence. But what he said wasn't cute, it wasn't a compliment, and it wasn't an intentional lesson. It was an insult. It is only through continued advocacy, that she changes Jesus' mind and she—the foreign woman—becomes the only person in scripture to correct Jesus appropriately.

What got into Jesus? Two important points are evident from this story. The first is that Jesus is clearly a bit worn down. He's been teaching constantly and wants and needs some time alone. If the gospel portrays his travel schedule with any accuracy, he was traveling nonstop and likely hadn't cared for himself. In doing so, he missed the point of his own message. The second point is that everyone, *even Jesus*, has unconscious biases. We are all a product of our individual environments, and the process of awakening is...a process. Ongoing. Just as being a Christian is an ongoing journey we strive to walk our whole lives, you don't just "get woke." Rather, "being woke" is a process of ongoing awakening and continual learning. It's also true that points one and two are connected in this story—that if we don't care for ourselves and we don't continue to stay alert to the injustices in society, we are likely to revert to our biases no matter how much work we've done to dismantle them. May we care for ourselves, so that we can truly care for each other. May it be so. Amen.

QUESTIONS

- How does it feel to see Jesus express a bias towards someone?

- When have you discovered that you are biased towards someone simply because of who they are or where they're from?

- What does it mean that a foreign woman corrects Jesus?

- In what specific areas of your life have you found yourself becoming more awakened?

- How does the environment in which you were raised inform how you see the world?

Spiritual Practice

During this section, we are highlighting women in the Bible. While countless women were undoubtedly written out of history, our literature, including the Bible, does give us some significant stories. In this week's centering scripture, we heard about a woman who had to advocate for herself. Another time when this happens is in the Book of Ruth. This week, read Ruth and take note of where you see her overcoming systems of oppression.

Video Reflection

Don't forget to scan the QR Code on the cover of this book for more on this topic and a mid-week spiritual practice.

Week 10 – Biblical Women: Creating a New Religion

....

Then [Hagar] went and sat down opposite him a good way off, about the distance of a bowshot, for she said, "Do not let me look on the death of the child." And as she sat opposite him, she lifted up her voice and wept. And God heard the voice of the boy, and the angel of God called to Hagar from heaven and said to her, "What troubles you, Hagar? Do not be afraid, for God has heard the voice of the boy where he is. Come, lift up the boy and hold him fast with your hand, for I will make a great nation of him." (Genesis 21:16–18)

We Christians would do well to spend more time with the story of Hagar. You probably remember the outline of the story. Abraham and Sarah are old and can't conceive a child. So, Sarah "gives" her handmaid Hagar to Abraham, and she gives birth to a son whom they named Ishmael. Then, against the odds, Sarah does, after all, become pregnant and has her own son, Isaac. Now, Sarah can't stand the sight of Hagar and Ishmael and asks Abraham to dismiss them, which he does by sending them out into the wilderness. We hear that God plans to make a great nation of Ishmael, that God provides them with some water, and that Ishmael grows up in the wilderness. And then Hagar and Ishmael disappear from the Judeo-Christian story with little worry about how Abraham and Sarah exploited and then abandoned Hagar.

Islam, on the other hand, has much to say about Hagar and Ishmael. Though not found in the Qur'an, the story of Hagar and Ishmael in the desert is expanded in Islamic tradition. While in the wilderness, both Hagar and Ishmael are about to die of thirst. To prevent this, Hagar runs back and forth between two hills searching for water. On the seventh trip, Hagar encounters an angel who delivers the message that God has heard their cries and will care for them. Then a spring of water bursts forth from the earth. It is Hagar's extreme effort, in a desperate circumstance, that prompts God's goodwill. In this version of the story, Abraham eventually returns and helps Ishmael build the Kaaba—the large black cube to which Muslims travel on their pilgrimage and is the most sacred site in Islam—as a reminder of the miracle Hagar and

Ishmael encountered in the wilderness.[3] When Muslims travel to Mecca, they walk around the Kaaba seven times, as a reminder of the seven trips that Hagar made in search of water. Whenever Muslims pray, they face in the direction of the Kaaba. The black stone in its middle is thought to have been brought by the angel Gabriel.[4]

In Islam, Hagar goes from being the discarded concubine to a woman of authority. She overcomes an incredibly difficult circumstance to become the matriarch of monotheism. Just as Judaism and Christianity trace their line through Sarah and Abraham's son Isaac, Islam traces its line through Hagar and Abraham's son Ishmael. Muhammad is said to be a descendant of Ishmael in the same way that Jesus is said to be a descendant of Isaac. Hagar's story reminds us that how we view people, places, and events is largely determined by who tells the story and what agenda they have. How often have we failed to understand something important because of how the story has been told? Aware of our lack of understanding, it makes sense to develop the habit of looking for situations where people are being excluded and to lift up voices that aren't being heard. May it be so. Amen.

QUESTIONS

*   When have you changed your opinion about something or someone after hearing the story from a different perspective?

*   Which groups of people are being excluded from our cultural story?

*   Who are some people in the Bible or in your own life who dealt with a difficult circumstance in a way that you find admirable?

*   What other common characteristics are there between Christianity and Islam?

---

3   Michael Molloy, *Experiencing The World's Religion's: Tradition, Challenge, and Change*, 3rd ed. (New York: McGraw-Hill, 2005), 439.

4   John L. Esposito, *Islam: The Straight Path* (Oxford: Oxford University Press, 2011), 112.

*   Judaism, Christianity, and Islam have many common characters and characteristics. What might be some repercussions if we focused on that common ground rather than on our differences?

Spiritual Practice

In Islam Hagar became a very significant figure due to her strength and determination. Another strong biblical figure is Esther. This week, make time to read the Book of Esther. The Jewish celebration of Purim often occurs during Women's History Month. Purim celebrates Esther's role and is an incredibly fun and meaningful celebration. If you're near a synagogue, consider attending one of these services.

Video Reflection

Don't forget to scan the QR Code on the cover of this book for more on this topic and a mid-week spiritual practice.

Week 11 – Biblical Women:
The Woman Who Showed Us How to Live

....

One of the Pharisees asked Jesus to eat with him, and when he
went into the Pharisee's house he reclined to dine. And a woman
in the city who was a sinner, having learned that he was eating
in the Pharisee's house, brought an alabaster jar of ointment.
She stood behind him at his feet, weeping, and began to bathe
his feet with her tears and to dry them with her hair, kissing
his feet and anointing them with the ointment. Now when
the Pharisee who had invited him saw it, he said to himself,
"If this man were a prophet, he would have known who and
what kind of woman this is who is touching him, that she is a
sinner." (Luke 7:36–39)

The scene in this week's centering scripture is incredibly radical.
Uninvited, a woman comes up to Jesus at a Pharisee's home. The
text says that she is a sinner, which means that a Pharisee—the
religious group that was incredibly concerned with the law—
would not have wanted her there. She brings a jar of ointment to
anoint Jesus. This was no mere foot cream, that we would think
of today. No; in the ancient world people used ointment to anoint
kings! That's exactly what Jesus was supposed to be. Jesus' followers
made the bold assertion that he was the Messiah. The Messiah
was understood to be a warrior-king who would lead a violent
revolution to overthrow the principalities and the powers—in this
case the Roman Empire—and to reestablish a United Kingdom of
Israel which he would then rule. By affirming Jesus as the Messiah,
Jesus' disciples were reinterpreting the term. Instead of a violent
revolution, Jesus was leading a nonviolent revolution of the heart
in which people proclaimed that their ultimate allegiance wasn't to
the Roman Empire, but to the Reign of God on Earth. Their loyalty
was to God, not Caesar. That was an incredibly radical statement
to make.

This woman recognizes Jesus as the Messiah and performs a ritual
anointment that should have been reserved for a king. She doesn't
pour the jar of ointment over his head, as would have been typical.
Instead, she uses the anointment on Jesus' feet. In her society,

touching someone's feet was a euphemism for sex. The fact that Jesus allowed a woman—who wasn't supposed to be touching a man who wasn't her husband—to anoint his feet was incredibly scandalous! It said an incredible amount about Jesus' ministry that he allowed this marginalized woman to anoint him as the Messiah—a sinner who boldly broke societal norms. His message was for people just like her. God was on the side of people who were like her. She was what the Reign of God looked like. The Pharisee host protested the whole incident, but it made no difference to Jesus. To him, the scene was a lesson about the value of the spirit of the law over the letter of the law. Love was the answer, and this act was an embodiment of love.

Not only does this woman anoint Jesus' feet with ointment, but she uses her hair (also scandalous, by the way) and her very tears. It's amazing to me that Jesus allowed this to happen. He recognized that this woman was what the Reign of God looked like and invited her to continue, even though the Pharisee was horrified by what he saw. This story reminds us of how God participates in our world. Jesus did not do what people expected of him. He proclaimed a radical vision for the future in which everyone had enough, the downtrodden were lifted, and the oppressed were set free. If we could envision, and proclaim that message, imagine how different our world would be. May it be so. Amen.

QUESTIONS

- What do you think it means that Jesus was willing to embrace something completely scandalous?

- What is scandalous for the Church today that we ought to be talking about?

- What do you think it signifies that a *woman* anointed Jesus?

- What role are women and should women be playing in the Church today?

- What would it look like for our society to get beyond a gender binary?

Spiritual Practice

Jesus was constantly defying social expectations when it came to gender roles. The longest one-on-one conversation that Jesus has in the gospels is his interaction with the woman at the well; found in John 4:1-42. Read the story this week and see what you notice about the interaction.

Video Reflection

Don't forget to scan the QR Code on the cover of this book for more on this topic and a mid-week spiritual practice.

Week 12 – Biblical Women: Making Jesus' Ministry Possible

....

Soon afterward [Jesus] went on through one town and village after another, proclaiming and bringing the good news of the kingdom of God. The twelve were with him, as well as some women who had been cured of evil spirits and infirmities: Mary, called Magdalene, from whom seven demons had gone out, and Joanna, the wife of Herod's steward Chuza, and Susanna, and many others, who ministered to them out of their own resources. (Luke 8:1–3)

Most modern scholars agree that Jesus' ministry would not have been possible without women. Not only did Jesus have women followers, but as we see from this scripture, Jesus was also funded by women. Jesus was an itinerant preacher who was entirely dependent upon the hospitality of others. Had it not been for the generosity of women supporters, he would not have been able to preach the gospel. Anyone who denies the role of women in the Church has not truly read the gospels, because in them we repeatedly see Jesus embracing the gifts of women and uplifting their gifts. Jesus' message showed an incredible welcome to those who were marginalized, including women. Those places in the later epistles that condemn women's leadership do so because Jesus' message was more radical than their culture allowed, and they felt like they needed to "tone it down a bit" by excluding women from leadership in the Church.

In Luke's Gospel, Jesus is more concerned than in any of the other gospels about those who are oppressed. It's not surprising that it is Luke who recognizes that women are helping Jesus. In this week's centering scripture, it's significant that these particular women are named. Luke recognizes the significant role that these women had in Jesus' ministry which is completely consistent with the way Jesus is portrayed throughout the gospel. What does it tell us that Jesus accepted resources from women? It tells us that even though society looked down upon an entire gender, Jesus recognized and embraced women's value as vital to ministry.

In the gospels, we see Jesus proclaiming constantly that God is a God of the margins. Our God is a God who cares about those who are being oppressed. If there is one thing that we can learn from following the teachings of Jesus, it's that we must side with those who are not being heard and advocate for them. That's probably why these women were funding Jesus in the first place. They were like first-century feminists who wanted their voices to be heard, their personhood to be recognized, and their values to be affirmed. Jesus did just that. Jesus proclaimed that in the Reign of God, absolutely everyone would be loved by God as they were—as equals. We must proclaim the same. May it be so. Amen,

QUESTIONS

- What does it mean that women were the primary funders of Jesus' ministry?

- If Jesus embraced women, why do you think the early Church subjugated them?

- In what ways does the Church continue to oppress women?

- In what ways does society continue to oppress women?

- How should Christians confront misogyny in the world?

Spiritual Practice

The women in this week's centering scripture funded Jesus' ministry, but Mary raised him! Read the first three chapters in the Gospel of Luke. How do they portray Mary? Pay particular attention to Mary's prayer in Luke 1:46–55. What effect do you think it had on Jesus to have a mother such as Mary?

Video Reflection

Don't forget to scan the QR Code on the cover of this book for more on this topic and a mid-week spiritual practice.

ECO-SPIRITUALITY

Week 13 – Eco-Spirituality: Original Blessing

....

God looked at all of this creation, and proclaimed that this was
good—very good...thus the heavens and the earth in all their
array were finished. (Genesis 1:31–2:1)[1]

It's odd to me that though the Bible so frequently focuses on
God's connection to nature, many Christians have a difficult time
understanding that we have a moral obligation to protect the Earth.
For us Christians, creation care ought to be a deeply spiritual act,
because God is made manifest through nature. The creation stories[2]
are the first narratives we read in the Bible, and they discuss God's
intimate connection with the Earth and all that is in it. These
stories were never meant to be a literal historical account of how
the Earth came to be, but rather are stories designed to make sense
of the world's etiology. Both creation stories strive to answer how
the world came to be, why humans exist, and why the human
condition is often precarious.

Many Christians dwell on the second creation story centered on
Adam and Eve, assuming a theology of "original sin" based on
centuries of Christian teaching. This theology—a later invention
by Christian theologians—misconstrues a story designed to give a
mythical understanding of why there is suffering in the world. The
result is an extremely toxic theology that portrays human beings
as fundamentally sinful. The first creation story gives us the much
more life-giving theology of "original blessing."[3] Original blessing
holds that after each act of creation, God looks at what has been
created and affirms it as good. The theology of original blessing
fundamentally shifts how we see ourselves and the world. We are
not inherently sinful and living in a world that is destined to be
destroyed. Instead, we have been fashioned and affirmed by God.
Likewise, the Earth is good, and we are good. We have been given

[1] Priests for Equality, *The Inclusive Bible: The First Egalitarian Transla-*
tion (Lanham, MD: Rowman & Littlefield, 2007).

[2] There are two creation stories. The first is Genesis 1:1–2:4a. The
second is Genesis 2:4b–25.

[3] Matthew Fox, *Original Blessing: A Primer in Creation Spirituality*
(Santa Fe: Bear & Company, 1983).

a sacred place to live and are called to inhabit this Earth joyfully and to see it as a gift with which we have been entrusted.

Some of us Christians also misinterpret v. 28 of the first creation story, a verse in which human beings are given "dominion" over the Earth to "subdue it." These Christians use the verse as an excuse to treat the Earth with little regard. After all, if we are given absolute control over the Earth, shouldn't we be able to do whatever we want with it? Such conclusions are dangerous and illogical. The first creation story explains the human desire to control nature in a fight for survival (the climate crisis and the prevalence of natural disasters have shown that despite technological advances, we still cannot tame nature). Some Christians take the idea of dominion even further and say that we ought to destroy the Earth to hasten the eschaton (end times). The whole concept of the end times results from misreading the Book of Revelation, which is truly about early Christian persecution—a misreading in which it is taken out of its historical context and allegory is presented as a prediction. If we Christians really want to be faithful, we ought to look at nature and say "God has made this good. God has made me good. Thanks be to God." May it be so. Amen.

QUESTIONS

- How does it change our theology to embrace the concept of "original blessing" over "original sin"?

- How does it feel to think about God creating you and affirming you as fundamentally good, instead of inherently flawed?

- Is nature spiritual for you? If so, how? If not, why?

- How are you involved in caring for God's creation?

- Where and when do you most fully experience God?

Spiritual Practice

Throughout this section on Eco-Spirituality, we will strive to spend time in God's creation rejoicing in God's presence. Think about one of your favorite outdoor places and go there if possible. If you can walk around, then spend time walking, breathing deeply, and taking in the beauty of nature. If you're not as mobile, sit somewhere outside or near a window and notice creation. If it's helpful, you might also add breathing meditation to your time in nature. Before you leave, say to yourself, "God has made this, and it is good."

Video Reflection

Don't forget to scan the QR Code on the cover of this book for more on this topic and a mid-week spiritual practice.

Week 14 - Eco-Spirituality: Environmental Racism

....

> Happy are those whose help is the God of Jacob, whose hope is
> in the LORD[4] their God, who made heaven and earth, the sea,
> and all that is in them; who keeps faith forever; who executes
> justice for the oppressed; who gives food to the hungry. The
> LORD sets the prisoners free; the LORD opens the eyes of the
> blind. The LORD lifts up those who are bowed down; the LORD
> loves the righteous. The LORD watches over the strangers; he
> upholds the orphan and the widow, but the way of the wicked
> he brings to ruin. (Psalm 146:5-10)

I love how Psalm 146 connects care for the Earth with other social
justice issues. The psalm begins with an appeal to praise God and
to burst forth in song. This doxology is an expression of ultimate
loyalty to God, and a reminder not to trust in the princes of the
world that follows it. The psalmist is pointing out the undeniable
fact that we cannot trust that those in positions of power will
automatically do the right thing because they often won't without
appropriate pressure. To recognize our responsibility to care for
others in God's call for justice is an act of faith. After all, our God is
the "God who made heaven and earth, the sea and all within it" and
who executes justice for the oppressed, gives food to the hungry,
sets prisoners free, lifts the downtrodden, and watches over the
widow, the orphan, and the stranger. This psalm expertly connects
ecology to spirituality and reminds us that they are intimately
intertwined; care of the Earth is as much a justice issue as caring
for the oppressed and those without enough.

Climate change is a reality that disproportionately affects
those who are living in poverty, especially those who depend
upon the land to survive. Extreme temperatures, flooding,
droughts, and environmental disasters affect food production
and sustainability. Environmental justice issues are not merely
limited to climate change, though. Environmental racism is also
an undeniable reality. One of the earliest and most tragic examples
of environmental racism in US history is when the government

---

[4] Whenever we see "The LORD" in our English translations of the
Hebrew Bible, it's actually God's proper name *Yahweh* often abbreviated
YHWH.

moved Indigenous Peoples from their ancestral lands to less desirable land, while also encouraging the over-hunting of bison to force Indigenous Peoples to western reservations. Exploitation of Native lands continues to this day; the Dakota Access Pipeline through Standing Rock is a case in point. Environmental racism isn't limited to the exploitation of native peoples, either. The Commission for Racial Justice (CRJ) of the United Church of Christ discovered in a study that the government had been intentionally selecting communities of color for waste disposal sites and polluting industrial facilities—essentially condemning them to contamination.[5] Let's not forget the water contamination in Flint, Michigan as a recent and very public example of how this kind of exploitation can happen. Environmental racism can be more covert, too, and can be as simple as a food desert.[6]

Eco-spirituality involves more than just acknowledging that the Earth is sacred; it also means looking to and addressing all the issues that are intertwined with the environment. God calls us to praise God for the Earth and to become co-creators with God in making the Earth a more just and peaceful place for all of creation. May it be so. Amen.

QUESTIONS

- When and where have you seen or experienced environmental racism?

- What are some ways to address environmental racism?

- With which environmental groups addressing environmental racism are you familiar? How have you encountered these groups?

- What other justice issues are related to the environment?

- What could you do to help make the Earth a more just and peaceful place?

---

[5] "Toxic Wastes and Race in the United States: A National Report on the Racial and Socio-Economic Characteristics of Communities with Hazardous Waste Sites" (United Church of Christ Commission for Racial Justice, 1987).

[6] A food desert is a community where there is limited or no access to affordable healthy food.

Spiritual Practice

Throughout this section on eco-spirituality, we will strive to spend time in God's creation rejoicing in God's presence. If you're able, take a walk (bike ride, bus ride, drive) around your community. Pay attention. Do you notice any food deserts? Who lives near the industrial areas and garbage dumps, the noisy highways, train tracks, and busy parking lots? Who lives under a flight path, or downwind from factory chimneys? How and where do you notice environmental racism?

Video Reflection

Don't forget to scan the QR Code on the cover of this book for more on this topic and a mid-week spiritual practice.

Week 15 – Eco-Spirituality: Lessons from Nature

"Therefore I tell you, do not worry about your life, what you will eat or what you will drink, or about your body, what you will wear. Is not life more than food and the body more than clothing? Look at the birds of the air: they neither sow nor reap nor gather into barns, and yet your heavenly Father feeds them. Are you not of more value than they? And which of you by worrying can add a single hour to your span of life? And why do you worry about clothing? Consider the lilies of the field, how they grow; they neither toil nor spin, yet I tell you, even Solomon in all his glory was not clothed like one of these. (Matthew 6:25-29)

Not worrying sounds great, but it's easier said than done, Jesus! It's a nice sentiment to hear that we shouldn't worry, but some of us have a real concern about having enough money to pay rent or mortgage, ensuring that there's enough food to eat, or about the medical test results for which we've been waiting. Sometimes worry is beyond our control and there are real things worth worrying about. We also know that some of us who live with mental illness literally cannot help but worry. Worrying is natural and it's not always possible to stop. On the other hand, we can "what if?" ourselves to death. We can spend so much time obsessing over "what ifs" that we can completely miss the reality in which we are living. We can obsess over "what if" this happens or "what if" that happens, and 99 percent of those worries will never come to fruition.

Many Eastern traditions remind us that the moment in which we find ourselves is the only moment that truly exists. That everything else—both past and future—is a creation of our imagination, seen through our interpretive lens. Jesus recognized this and saw grounding for this teaching within nature itself. Have you ever noticed how often Jesus points us towards nature when teaching? He taught outside, used familiar analogies for those who depended upon the land, and reminded us of our connection to creation. In this week's lesson, Jesus suggests that by looking to nature, we find a source of grounding. The birds go about their work without stopping to worry whether they will have enough, and God provides. The lilies grow without worrying whether their petals will be beautiful, and they are radiant. We have much to learn from nature, which is why Jesus consistently points us towards it.

Being mindful of the moment does not solve our problems, but there is increasing evidence that slowing down and focusing on breathing and one discreet task at a time can help with our anxiety—even for those of us who have anxiety disorders. If we believe that nature is sacred and that God is within all of creation, then perhaps there is something to be said for facilitating a greater connection with the natural world and taking time to consider the birds and the lilies. While being outdoors may not cause all anxiety to cease, perhaps we will discover that today's worries are enough for today and that tomorrow's worries can wait until tomorrow. May it be so. Amen.

QUESTIONS

- Think about some of the worries that you've had over the past week. How many of them legitimately warranted concern?

- What would it feel like to let go of the worries that are out of your control?

- How do you feel when you spend time in nature? Is your anxiety level different?

- What lessons have you learned from spending time in nature?

- Sometimes acknowledging our worries can help to reduce anxiety even if there's nothing that we can do to resolve them. What are some concerns in your life that you're legitimately worried about right now?

Spiritual Practice

Throughout this section on eco-spirituality, we will strive to spend time in God's creation rejoicing in God's presence. If you're able, go outside and find somewhere peaceful and quiet. Pay attention to the sounds that you hear. Are there birds singing, crickets chirping, water flowing? Pay attention to the sights that you see, as well. Are there flowers? Clouds? Of what type? What colors and shapes? What lessons can you learn from the creation that you are observing?

Video Reflection

Don't forget to scan the QR Code on the cover of this book for more on this topic and a mid-week spiritual practice.

Week 16 – Eco-Spirituality: Planting Seeds

....

"Listen! A sower went out to sow. And as he sowed, some seed fell on a path, and the birds came and ate it up. Other seed fell on rocky ground, where it did not have much soil, and it sprang up quickly, since it had no depth of soil. And when the sun rose, it was scorched, and since it had no root it withered away. Other seed fell among thorns, and the thorns grew up and choked it, and it yielded no grain. Other seed fell into good soil and brought forth grain, growing up and increasing and yielding thirty and sixty and a hundredfold." (Mark 4:3–8)

In seminary, I took a class called "World Religions and Ecology" in which we talked about the potential that all religious traditions have for both positive and negative environmental impact, depending upon which texts are read and how the religious traditions are leveraged. Unfortunately, I quickly discovered that Christianity was one of the worst offenders of environmental exploitation. It immediately struck me that Christians who were bad environmentalists had fundamentally missed the point of Jesus' message, which is that all that is around us is sacred and is from God. In caring for creation, we are fulfilling the two greatest commandments, to love God and our neighbors.

The more that I sat with that realization, the more that I recognized that caring for the environment is a fundamental faith issue and that if we aren't claiming God's creation as sacred, we aren't being faithful. Throughout the gospels, Jesus uses a variety of agricultural parables, but none is more poignant for me than that of the Sower. This parable is found in all the synoptic gospels and the Gospel of Thomas. Since it is attested in both Thomas and Mark, this parable is very likely to have originated with the historical Jesus and not later editors/theologians.[7] While the Parable of the Sower is about spreading the gospel, I think this can also be applied to modern-day climate concerns.

---

[7] Historical Jesus scholars call sayings of Jesus that come from sources that were written independently "multiple independent attestation." Since these sayings come from more than one source, they are more likely to have come from Jesus than from later editors.

We reap what we sow, don't we? If we continue environmental disregard at this pace, the Earth will not be here for future generations, for we will quite literally bring about the apocalypse! But if we recognize that our actions have consequences and begin making immediate changes, we might be able to save this world that God so loves. Individuals and organizations need to make efforts to reduce their carbon footprints, but let's be realistic: what truly needs to happen to ensure a sustainable future is long-term, radical systemic change. Corporations are primarily responsible for the majority of pollution and environmental degradation. If we want to make an impact, we need our governments to regulate industry in an environmentally conscious way. Our individual actions have a minimal effect—even collectively. We need to use our voting power to get people into office who will implement environmental restrictions on the most obvious offenders while ensuring that the products to which we have access are environmentally sustainable. Make the changes that you can make, of course, but fight for systemic change that ensures that the Earth will be here for generations to come. If we do that, our grandchildren may benefit from the seeds that we are sowing now. May it be so. Amen.

QUESTIONS

- Do you think the environmental crisis is one of accumulative harms (all of us doing a little bit of harm that adds up) or do you agree that large corporations are primarily responsible for exploiting the environment?

- What would a solution to the environmental crisis look like from your perspective?

- What benefits of the "seeds" we are planting for environmental justice might we see in our lifetime?

- What are the most urgent environmental concerns that we need to address?

- What other scriptures lend themselves to thinking about environmental justice?[8]

Spiritual Practice

Throughout this section on eco-spirituality, we have spent time in God's creation rejoicing in God's presence. If you're able, sit next to a tree or plant that has taken many years to grow. Otherwise, imagine one. Spend a few moments in meditation thinking about the time necessary for you and that piece of creation to be present together. What was involved in that plant being there? What acts of protection had to be undertaken for you both to be in the same space? What would the landscape be like if the plant were gone? What seeds for environmental justice can you plant now?

Video Reflection

Don't forget to scan the QR Code on the cover of this book for more on this topic and a mid-week spiritual practice.

---

[8] A great resource for thinking about environmental interpretations is *The Green Bible*, in which all ecological scripture is printed in green.

MENTAL HEALTH

Week 17 – Mental Health: Beyond the Bible

As the sun was setting, all those caring for any who were sick with various kinds of diseases brought them to him, and he laid his hands on each of them and cured them. (Luke 4:40)

Let's begin by acknowledging that the Bible does not understand mental health in the same way that we do today. The Bible doesn't understand *any* health issues in the way that we do today, because all the authors were writing in a pre-scientific world. That means that to make sense of the ailments both physical and mental that existed in their time, they had to use the language that they had available to them. As you can imagine that language does not equate to our current understanding of mental or physical health. Indeed, we are living in a time of great scientific advancement in which our understanding of how our bodies work is changing daily. Think about how many medical advancements have been made in the past decade, the past half-century, and the past century. It's almost unfathomable that all these advancements have been made in such a short time span.

One clear thing is that Jesus is portrayed as a healer throughout the gospels. We can go a couple of ways with that knowledge. Some Christians take Jesus' healing ministry to mean that he wants to be the healer of every ill and that if you pray hard enough to him, any ailment from which you suffer is not beyond his healing grasp. That's atrocious theology that leads to all types of morally problematic scenarios. For instance, what if someone has led a good life, caring for others, and is very faithful; yet no matter how hard they pray, they continue to suffer? When we read about Jesus being a healer in the ancient world, I don't think we should assume that anything supernatural is happening. Instead, we can assume that Jesus was practicing the medicine of his day and trying to help everyone that he could. In Jesus' world, people's physical and mental health were understood to be intertwined with spiritual health. If a person had leprosy, for instance, people assumed that they had been afflicted with a physical illness because something was wrong with their spiritual health. Of course, we now know how flawed such reasoning is, yet many Christians still believe it in their heart of hearts. We might wonder, would I be suffering if I were more faithful? If I pray hard enough, maybe my illness will disappear, and I'll be healed.

I don't think we get a promise of supernatural healing from the Bible, but I do think we find instructions about how we are to address the health challenges that we experience. Jesus didn't turn anyone away, even people who were ostracized by society because of their condition. Jesus never charged for his services but helped people in need because it was the right thing to do—this is certainly a lesson from which we can learn given the outrageous costs to access mental and physical health services in the US. Jesus helped people with their spiritual health while engaging with their physical and mental suffering. In doing so, he affirmed that they were loved by God and had not been abandoned. God does not promise to heal our ailments, but God does promise to be with us every step of the way. May it be so. Amen.

QUESTIONS

- What do you make of Jesus' healing ministry in the gospels?

- When you've had health struggles, have you felt God's presence?

- Can you think of people who have helped you feel God's love when you were in need?

- How do you make sense of theodicy (the fact that there's suffering in the world)?

- Are there ways that learning from Jesus can help us through challenging times?

Spiritual Practice

Throughout this section on mental health, we will focus on mindfulness practices. Sometimes life can feel overwhelming. Centering yourself for a moment can mitigate that feeling. Today, go to a favorite spot. It can be inside or outside, at home or somewhere else, physically or in your imagination. Sit down somewhere that's comfortable and spend a few moments with your eyes closed, focusing on your breath. Open your eyes and pay attention to what is around you. What do you see? What do you hear? Are there things that you haven't noticed before? Sometimes in our busyness, we overlook the details. Try to be present in the moment and observe what is happening.

Video Reflection

Don't forget to scan the QR Code on the cover of this book for more on this topic and a mid-week spiritual practice.

Week 18 – Mental Health: Dealing with Our Demons

....

> *That evening, at sunset, they brought to him all who were*
> *sick or possessed by demons. And the whole city was gathered*
> *around the door. And he cured many who were sick with various*
> *diseases and cast out many demons, and he would not permit*
> *the demons to speak, because they knew him. (Mark 1:32–34)*

In Mark's Gospel, Jesus performs *many* exorcisms. The story in this week's centering scripture isn't even the first exorcism that Jesus has performed in the gospel's opening chapter. There's quite a bit going on with these exorcisms, and none of them should be taken to mean that a demon literally possessed a person. Many of these passages speak more metaphorically about the power of Jesus' message to drive out personal and systemic evil. However, I think that once we've adopted a metaphorical approach, we can recognize that the stories can be helpful tools for thinking about mental health.

We know that one in five adults in the United States lives with mental illness.[1] Diagnosed mental illness statistics are likely underreported due to the stigma that still exists surrounding mental health. Some of these mental illnesses are manageable with support and medication, and some are much more difficult to regulate. Of these one-in-five Americans who live with mental illness, some suffer from Serious Mental Illness, which the National Institute of Mental Health defines as "a mental, behavioral, or emotional disorder resulting in serious functional impairment, which substantially interferes with or limits one or more major life activities."[2] Serious Mental Illness affects 5.5% of all US adults.[3]

People two thousand years ago didn't have the scientific knowledge to diagnose mental health issues that we have today, so they needed to use the terminology that was available to them. One of the ways

---

[1] National Institute on Mental Health (NAMI), "Mental Illness," 2023, https://www.nimh.nih.gov/health/statistics/mental-illness#:~:text=Mental%20illnesses%20are%20common%20in,(57.8%20million%20in%202021).

[2] NAMI, "Mental Illness," 2023.

[3] NAMI, "Mental Illness," 2023.

that they commonly described a person acting in a way that was out of the norm was as someone who a demon had possessed. When we read stories about demonic possession, one possible interpretation is that someone with a Serious Mental Illness approached Jesus and asked for help. I do not believe in magical healings, but I do think that it's significant that the Bible portrays Jesus as helping people who were suffering. Reading this with our twenty-first century eyes, I think we can say that just as Jesus desired those who approached him to be healed, God also desires us to live happy and healthy lives. One way we can do that is to pay attention to our mental health and recognize when we need help. If we are feeling down, anxious, or afraid and we get stuck, God desires us to reach out for help. It may begin with a call to a loved one. It may include therapy or medication, and that is nothing to be ashamed of! After all, God wants us to be happy, healthy people. May it be so. Amen.

QUESTIONS

- What would it feel like to believe that God wants us to be happy and healthy?

- Are there areas in your life that need a mental health check-up?

- Who are the loved ones you can turn to for support during difficult times?

- How can we dismantle the stigma surrounding mental health?

- How can you support someone who is struggling with mental health issues?

Spiritual Practice

Throughout this section on mental health, we will focus on mindfulness practices. Sometimes it can be easy to fixate on negative feelings and emotions. It can help to take a few moments to focus on the positive things in your life. Take a moment and think about those things in your life for which you are grateful. Then think about the things that you enjoy doing. If it's helpful, write them down. Perhaps even start a gratitude journal (I keep one on my phone so I can add things as they happen and go back and look at them when I need a boost).

Video Reflection

Don't forget to scan the QR Code on the cover of this book for more on this topic and a mid-week spiritual practice.

Week 19 – Mental Health: Laying down Our Burdens

....

Come to me, all you who are weary and are carrying heavy burdens, and I will give you rest. Take my yoke upon you, and learn from me, for I am gentle and humble in heart, and you will find rest for your souls. For my yoke is easy, and my burden is light. (Matthew 11:28–30)

In seminary I worked for an outdoor church that served the city's homeless population. The idea was that people could come and be fed spiritually and bodily. We had a short thirty-minute service that was designed with our houseless neighbors in mind, and then we shared a meal. This was *not* like many of the churches I've seen that want to exchange food for conversion. People didn't need to come to the service to get the food, but neither did we assume that people didn't have spiritual needs just because they lived outside. It was an incredibly powerful ministry that built community across socio-economic lines and was one of the most palpable expressions of the Reign of God I have ever seen.

Many of the folks who attended these services had problems that were beyond—yet tied to—their homelessness: serious mental illness, addiction, and estrangement from family were common features of many of their personal stories. Each week during the service we had a liturgy that was specifically crafted to be meaningful for people with similar struggles. For example, we recited the serenity prayer each week for those who were in recovery. We also heard this week's centering scripture at every service. For an entire year, this scripture was repeated weekly as I sat with people going through incredibly difficult times. I sat with people, shared meals; and heard stories of hope and loss, joy and pain, success, and failure. I began to recognize that this—a ragtag group of struggling people—is what the beloved community looks like.

I also recognized that there is a promise throughout the Bible— which for Christians is made manifest in the person of Jesus—that we are never alone and will never be abandoned by a God who loves us more than anything. With that knowledge, I have repeatedly found peace and rest for my soul. God does not promise that life will be easy or that everything will go our way. God does promise to be with us every step, each day. Perhaps God's presence looks like being there for a loved one. Perhaps, it looks like a faith community mourning the loss of a beloved child of God. Perhaps, it looks like shouting that we've had enough and need a change in our lives. Whatever the case, God *does not* and *will not* abandon us. God desires that we find rest for our souls. May it be so. Amen.

QUESTIONS

- What situations in your life feel overwhelming right now?

- What would it feel like to lay down your suffering before God?

- How have you found peace and rest for your soul when you've needed it most?

- When have you felt abandoned by God?

- What does it feel like to know that God has promised to be with you no matter what you've done, or what you're going through?

Spiritual Practice

Throughout this section on mental health, we will focus on mindfulness practices. Take a moment to close your eyes. Try to discern how you are feeling at this moment. Acknowledge those feelings. To what or whom do you feel most connected at this moment? What would it feel like to think of that connection as God made manifest? Perhaps if you feel distant from God, you can try this spiritual practice to reestablish a connection.

Video Reflection

Don't forget to scan the QR Code on the cover of this book for more on this topic and a mid-week spiritual practice.

Week 20 – Mental Health: Anxiety

....

Cast all your anxiety on him, because he cares for you.
(1 Peter 5:7)

Here's what I don't think this scripture is saying: If you trust in God, all your anxiety will fade away. Many churches preach that if you have strong enough faith, all your troubles will fade away. That's terrible theology! Faith does not heal us, but it can be a tool for helping us to deal with the difficulties that we encounter. I don't often read 1 Peter, but I think this verse is helpful. It comes in the context of advice to people who are leaders in the church and may feel unsure about their qualifications for leadership. I think that it's universally applicable. Recognizing that we are feeling anxious, acknowledging our anxiety as real, and remembering that God cares about us is itself an anxiety-reducing process.

One of the greatest cultural deceptions involves deluding ourselves into thinking that if we ignore something long enough it will just go away. It won't. If we are feeling anxious about something, it is our mind telling us that we are concerned about an issue. I recently heard a story on NPR about how feeling anxious was helpful, evolutionarily, because our bodies needed to make us feel uncomfortable when we were in danger. It was this sense that helped us to survive as a species. However, as time has progressed, most of us don't have to worry as much about being eaten by a dangerous animal, but our primitive mind is still on full alert. This means that if we say something out of turn, for instance, that is interpreted in a hurtful way by someone else, our anxiety ramps up as if our lives were literally in danger. If this is experienced often it becomes impossible to deal with. For some people, that anxiety is beyond control and must be regulated with medicine and/or therapy.

Our human brains are so incredibly complex that we are just scratching the surface of the science behind how they work. Yet one thing is clear: caring for our mental health is just as serious as caring for our physical health. God will not magically get rid of our anxiety, depression, or apprehension with a prayer. How we feel is connected with how we're wired at a biological level. Recognizing how we are feeling and acknowledging that God is with us can be very comforting. May we accept that God cares for us and make every effort to care for ourselves, too. May it be so. Amen.

QUESTIONS

- What are you anxious about in your life right now?

- Do you tend to acknowledge such feelings, or do you ignore them?

- When you feel anxious or depressed, what do you do to help yourself feel better?

- What kinds of situations make you anxious?

- What makes you feel joyful?

Spiritual Practice

Throughout this section on mental health, we will focus on mindfulness practices. This week let's try a body scan where we will pay attention to how our bodies feel. Sit in a comfortable position and close your eyes. Focus on your breath as you breathe in and out. After a few moments, begin to take notice of how your body is feeling. Begin with your toes and work your way up. Focus on physical sensations. Do your toes tingle or feel numb? Are your hips or your back sore? Can you feel air blowing on your skin? Our mental health can often have physical manifestations. Body scanning can help us to connect with our bodies and ground us in the present.

Video Reflection

Don't forget to scan the QR Code on the cover of this book for more on this topic and a mid-week spiritual practice.

LGBTQ+ INCLUSION

Week 21 – LGBTQ+ Inclusion: Hope Hidden in the Text

For there are eunuchs who have been so from birth, and there are eunuchs who have been made eunuchs by others, and there are eunuchs who have made themselves eunuchs for the sake of the kingdom of heaven. Let anyone accept this who can. (Matthew 19:12)

Whereas people often use the Bible to oppress others, Jesus gave us the criterion of love, and all the theology and biblical interpretation that we do must pass the test of love or else it is incompatible with the teachings of Jesus. I would go so far as to say that any hateful message is anti-Christian. We Christians have certainly been responsible for much of the oppression of the LGBTQ+ community in the US, and in so doing we've acted contrary to the teachings of Jesus, which are centered on love. On social media, I've challenged people to name a single teaching from Jesus that was anti-LGBTQ+ and they can't, because Jesus never mentioned it. In part, that's because the ancient understanding of sexual orientation and gender identity was different from our modern understanding, and he couldn't have addressed the current understanding because it didn't exist yet.

Even so, if you know the socio-historical context of passages, Jesus' message of radical inclusion can come from deep within the text. This week's centering scripture is buried within a teaching on divorce.[1] Here, Jesus mentions three types of eunuchs. The first includes those who have chosen to be eunuchs for the sake of the Reign of God. These are people who abstain from romantic relationships to focus on their relationship with God. Examples are priests, monks, and those who belong to religious orders. The second category consists of people who have been made eunuchs by others. These are men who have been castrated to remove their sexual desire so that they could be guards in a harem or

---

[1] When Jesus condemns divorce, he's doing it because it was a justice issue for the woman. A man could dismiss his wife for something as trivial as burning dinner and divorce would leave the woman without resources. Setting the requirement for divorce so high was meant to protect women in this ancient society and has little to do with our modern understandings of marriage and divorce.

for important women, without those women and their families worrying about the guards impregnating them. The third category is the one in which we are particularly interested here: those who have been eunuchs since birth. While the first two categories are speaking about those who abstain from romantic relationships, queer theologians point out that it is possible that those who have been eunuchs from birth are those who were born having natural, God-given desires to be with someone of the same gender or that they have deviated from societal expectations on sexual orientation/gender identity. Since their goal in a sexual relationship was not procreation, they were considered eunuchs. If this is the case, in an act of subversion that is all too easily overlooked, Jesus has blessed the LGBTQ+ community, himself. Moreover, you'll remember that in Acts 8, it was a eunuch who was the first gentile to be baptized—suggesting that the first outsider to be welcomed into the body of Christ might have been gay.

Sometimes we might wish that the Bible spoke more directly to modern social justice issues, but the text is confined to the understanding available at the time it was written. However, if we make the effort to understand Jesus' teachings on love and compassion and allow that to inform our reading of the text, we can see the love of God shine through the pages of the Bible and throughout the centuries. May we proclaim that love as loudly as we can, especially when so many people are misrepresenting the gospel. The gospel is clear: everybody's in, nobody's out. May it be so. Amen.

QUESTIONS

- Though the gospel goal is for everybody to be in and nobody to be out, whom are we currently excluding from the Christian community?

- If the authors of the Bible didn't have the same understanding that we have today of sexual orientation and gender identity, are the texts still relevant, and in what way?

- What would it look like to interpret even difficult texts through the criterion of love that Jesus gave to us?

- If there are ever limits to inclusion, what are they?

- If you're a part of a faith community, how can it live more fully into welcoming all?

Spiritual Practice

In this section, we'll reflect on quotations from members of the LGBTQ+ community. Dr. Emilie Townes, Dean Emerita at Vanderbilt Divinity School said, "I think we must wrestle with scripture and we often don't. We want to come up with something that more rubber stamps our opinion as opposed to looking at the complicated world of the Bible."[2] Spend some time with her words and engage them: journal, think about them, and have a conversation with someone about them. Why do we tend to look for ways to rubberstamp our own opinion? In what ways do we allow scripture to form our opinions?

Video Reflection

Don't forget to scan the QR Code on the cover of this book for more on this topic and a mid-week spiritual practice.

---

[2] Pete Enns, "The Bible for Normal People," n.d., https://thebiblefor-normalpeople.com/episode-228-emilie-townes-the-wisdom-of-hope-reissue/.

Week 22 – LGBTQ+ Inclusion: David and Jonathan

When David had finished speaking to Saul, the soul of Jonathan was bound to the soul of David, and Jonathan loved him as his own soul. (1 Samuel 18:1)

I am distressed for you, my brother Jonathan; greatly beloved were you to me; your love to me was wonderful, passing the love of women. (2 Samuel 1:26)

Whenever people say that there's no example of a same-gender relationship in the Bible, queer theologians often point to David and Jonathan. Were they just friends? Possibly. Were they lovers? Likely. There are at least six highly erotic passages about David and Jonathan, like in our centering scriptures from 1 and 2 Samuel.[3] David and Jonathan's deep love for one another seems to go beyond even a deep friendship. These verses describe an erotic love that surpasses "the love of women" and binds their two souls together. The concept of homosexuality didn't exist until the nineteenth century, but that doesn't mean that the LGBTQ+ community didn't exist. Instead, sexual orientation and gender identity simply weren't understood in the same way that we understand them today in the US. What we seem to find in the story of David and Jonathan is what we might expect in a loving, consensual same-gender relationship in our modern world.

It's true that David was married to several women (and the story of his rape of Bathsheba is a whole other morally problematic mess), but it's possible that he was either bisexual or simply married to women since marriage between men and women was the normative social structure at the time and being fully devoted to another man wouldn't have been socially acceptable. David's relationship with Jonathan also seems to be significantly healthier than his relationship with women. While the understanding of sexuality in the ancient Near East was different than our modern understanding, there was a recognition and acceptance of same-

---

[3] Susan Ackerman, *When Heroes Love: The Ambiguity of Eros in the Stories of Gilgamesh and David* (New York: Columbia University Press, 2005), 166.

gender sexual acts as a natural part of life for many people at the time. In fact, the language in 1 and 2 Samuel is like that of other homoerotic poetry in ancient Near Eastern literature.[4] Same-gender sexual relationships were certainly common in Greco-Roman culture, as well.[5]

In general, the Bible doesn't tend to be a great guide for romantic relationships, because the culture was so different that its advice on such relationships is almost irrelevant. Even the types of marriage described in the Bible are often outside of our cultural norms. While we probably shouldn't look to ancient texts to define modern relationships and romantic love (*eros* in Greek), the Bible can be a helpful guide for love of neighbor (*agape* in Greek). In the case of Jonathan and David, we find a consensual same-gender relationship with love and respect at its heart. In our lives, we ought to look for relationships—romantic or platonic—that are like that. For a relationship to be truly healthy, there must be unconditional acceptance, care for another beyond oneself, and a desire for the other to flourish. As we create relationships in our lives, those values should be the measure of the relationship. May it be so. Amen.

QUESTIONS

- What do you make of David and Jonathan's relationship?

- Are there other relationships in the Bible that challenge society's views of what's acceptable?

- What do you think about using the Bible to define modern relationships?

- Read through the story of David and Jonathan. Does it change your notion of what a romantic relationship can look like?

- Queer theology looks for LGBTQ+ themes in the Bible. Do other stories come up for you that might be

---

[4] Tom M. Horner, *Jonathan Loved David: Homosexuality in Biblical Times* (Louisville: The Westminster John Knox Press, 1978), 19.

[5] The exploitation of younger men by older men is at least partly at play in the verses that Paul writes about same gender sex in his epistles.

meaningful if considered through a queer theological lens?

Spiritual Practice

In this section, we'll reflect on quotations from members of the LGBTQ+ community. James Baldwin wrote, "You think your pain and your heartbreak are unprecedented in the history of the world, but then you read. It was books that taught me that the things that tormented me most were the very things that connected me with all the people who were alive, who had ever been alive."[6] Spend some time with that quotation and engage with it: journal and think about it, have a conversation with someone about it. How does reading the story of David and Jonathan make you feel? Are there stories in the Bible to which you can relate? Are there biblical characters to whom you feel a connection?

Video Reflection

Don't forget to scan the QR Code on the cover of this book for more on this topic and a mid-week spiritual practice.

---

[6] James Baldwin, "The Doom and Glory of Knowing Who You Are," *Life Magazine*, May 24, 1963.

Week 23 – LGBTQ+ Inclusion: The Spirit of the Law

....

> *Such is the confidence that we have through Christ toward God. Not that we are qualified of ourselves to claim anything as coming from us; our qualification is from God, who has made us qualified to be ministers of a new covenant, not of letter but of spirit, for the letter kills, but the Spirit gives life. (2 Corinthians 3:4-6)*

Paul was often harsh in his letters. He founded churches and when he felt that they were out of line, he chastised them for not following his teachings. A frequent refrain in Paul's letters is that he believes people have missed the point of the law. He had once been a Pharisee and freely admitted that he was also guilty of the same fallacy. Further, he believed that gentile converts to Christianity were not bound by the law and felt strongly that they should not adhere to it.[7] For this reason, he told people to embrace the spirit of the law, instead of the letter of the law. The religious law of the time was designed to help people draw closer to God, but by getting so concerned with enforcing the details of the law (as the Pharisees were wont to do) people were being driven further from God. Paul encourages his readers to embrace the reason why the law was put into place: to help us love God and love one another. If we do that, we are fulfilling the spirit of the law. That is why Jesus said he didn't come to abolish the law and the prophets but to fulfill both.

Many modern fundamentalist Christians miss the spirit of the Bible by striving to enforce the letter of the Bible. Moreover, they often don't understand the details of what's being described in the scripture that they're trying to enforce! The scriptures that they use to condemn LGBTQ+ people they take out of context and manipulate to reinforce homophobia and transphobia. Let me take you on a brief survey of the so-called *clobber passages* often used against the LGBTQ+ community to show you what I mean.

---

[7] A prime example of this is when Paul tells the church in Galatians 5:11-12 that if any male chooses to undergo circumcision that he hopes the knife slips and they castrate themselves!

- The story of Sodom and Gomorrah is not about condemning consensual same-gender relationships: it condemns an act of sexual violence. It was designed to show how far the people of Sodom had strayed. Instead of protecting the people to whom they had an obligation to extend hospitality, they actively wanted to harm them.[8] Further, the Book of Ezekiel explains that the sin of the people of Sodom was that they "had pride, excess of food, and prosperous ease but did not aid the poor and needy."[9]

- The Levitical laws that seemingly prohibit same-gender sexual relationships are quite unclear.[10] Some scholars suggest that they are condemning the practice of temple prostitution that may have been common in Canaanite temples.[11] Others suggest that the condemnation had to do with ensuring that there was a property heir and that every male sexual encounter needed to have the possibility for procreation, and that's why lesbian sexual relationships are not condemned.[12] Whatever the case, the Levitical laws were clearly not speaking about our modern conception of consensual same-gender relationships. Moreover, Leviticus tells us that it is for Israel (which is both culturally and geographically defined), so these laws are, by definition, not applicable to twenty-first-century Christians. That's why no one gets upset when other Levitical laws are broken, like laws about eating shellfish or wearing clothes made from more than one material. They're irrelevant for twenty-first-century life.[13]

---

[8] Story found in Genesis 19:1–38.

[9] Ezekiel 16:49.

[10] Amy-Jill Levine, "Amy-Jill Levine: How to Read the Bible's 'Clobber Passages' on Homosexuality," *Outreach* (blog), September 12, 2022, https://outreach.faith/2022/09/amy-jill-levine-how-to-read-the-bibles-clobber-passages-on-homosexuality/.

[11] Levine, ""Amy-Jill Levine: How to Read the Bible's 'Clobber Passages' on Homosexuality."

[12] Levine, ""Amy-Jill Levine: How to Read the Bible's 'Clobber Passages' on Homosexuality."

[13] These laws can be found in Leviticus 18:22, 20:13.

- Paul's condemnation of same-gender relationships in Romans 1 had to do with his teachings on power dynamics in the body of Christ. Paul believed that everyone ought to be on equal footing once they were a part of the body of Christ. In Hellenistic culture, it was common for older men to develop a sexual relationship with younger men, who often were not able to consent. Paul found that practice abhorrent because it was contrary to his beliefs about equality.[14]

There are other passages that fundamentalists sometimes use as clobber passages, passages that depend on words used in specific translations. But the above texts tend to be the main ones. The Bible is fundamentally about God's extravagant love for us and our calling to extend that love to our fellow human beings. Any reading of the biblical text that applies it differently may be enforcing the letter of the Bible, but certainly not the spirit. May we be people who embody this spirit every day. May it be so. Amen.

Spiritual Practice

Bishop Gene Robinson has said, "It's funny, isn't it, that you can preach a judgmental, and vengeful, and angry God, and nobody will mind. But if you start preaching about a God that is too accepting, too loving, too forgiving, too merciful, too kind — you are in trouble!"[15] Spend some time with that quotation and engage with it: journal, think about it, and have a conversation about it. Why do you think people so often interpret the Bible in hateful ways? What are ways that we can better embody God's radically inclusive love, communally and individually?

Video Reflection

Don't forget to scan the QR Code on the cover of this book for more on this topic and a mid-week spiritual practice.

---

[14] Paul's text can be found in Romans 1:25–27.
[15] *Act As If...*, Sermon (All Saints Church, Pasadena, 2016), https://www.youtube.com/watch?v=0ttMLXcTuiA&t=50s.

Week 24 - LGBTQ+ Inclusion: A God of Love

....

Beloved, let us love one another, because love is from God;
everyone who loves is born of God and knows God. Whoever
does not love does not know God, for God is love...Love has
been perfected among us in this: that we may have boldness
on the day of judgment, because as he is, so are we in this
world. There is no fear in love, but perfect love casts out fear;
for fear has to do with punishment, and whoever fears has not
reached perfection in love. We love because he first loved us.
Those who say, "I love God," and hate a brother or sister are
liars, for those who do not love a brother or sister, whom they
have seen, cannot love God, whom they have not seen. (1 John
4:7-8, 17-20)

The author of 1 John[16] understands that Jesus' entire message was about love, and the author spells it out for us in this scripture. Love is from God and if we don't know love then we don't truly know God. Then he nails it by saying, "There is no fear in love." All the "isms" and "phobias" that are present in our society are fundamentally about fear. Racism is about fear of someone who looks different. Sexism is about the fear that another gender might have power and autonomy. Homophobia is fear of someone who has a different sexual orientation. Transphobia is about fear of someone who is living into their authentic gender identity. Fear of the other is what inspires hate.

While it sounds odd, fear was (and often remains) evolutionarily beneficial. One of the reasons that we have survived as a species is because of fear—avoiding those who were different—taught our ancestors how to survive potential threats. While it might be biologically natural to seek out those who are similar and avoid those who are different, it is also entirely contrary to the teachings of Jesus, and it must be confronted with every fiber of our being. If we truly want to accept others, we cannot fear them. We must cast out our fear and embrace love if we truly want to follow Jesus.

---

[16] This is a different author than the Gospel of John or the John who wrote the Book of Revelation. None of the authors are Jesus' disciple John.

This is always something toward which we strive, but the best way to get better at courageous love is to practice it. If we encounter someone who is different and we feel uncomfortable, it is helpful to develop the practice of stopping and asking ourselves why we are feeling discomfort. Let's take the time to be mindful, to notice how we are feeling, and to counter any fear that we have with love. It's biblical!

The biblical author ends the section by suggesting we should love others *because God loved us first*. He then expands on that by saying that we can't expect to be able to love a God truly whom we cannot see if we can't love the human being sitting next to us. The author is spot on. The way that we love God is by loving our neighbors first. Begin with love! If we can love one another for who they are—those innate qualities about them like their sexual orientation and gender identity—then we are loving God, because we are all reflections of God and created in God's image. May it be so. Amen.

Spiritual Practice

Trans priest Fr. Shannon Kearns wrote, "If what it means to be righteous means being like them, I am not at all interested. I will claim my deviance with pride because to me my deviance looks an awful lot like trying to follow Jesus."[17] Spend some time with that quotation and engage with it: journal, think about it, and converse with someone about it. In what ways does the popular narrative of Christianity not coincide with the actual life and teachings of Jesus? What does it mean to follow Jesus, particularly when it means going against "orthodox" Christian teachings?

Video Reflection

Don't forget to scan the QR Code on the cover of this book for more on this topic and a mid-week spiritual practice.

---

[17] Shannon Kearns, "I Am A Deviant," *Queer Theology* (blog), n.d., https://www.queertheology.com/i-am-a-deviant/.

REIGN OF GOD

Week 25 –Reign of God: God, not Empire

....

*Now after John was arrested, Jesus came to Galilee, proclaiming
the good news of God, and saying, "The time is fulfilled, and
the kingdom of God has come near; repent, and believe in the
good news." (Mark 1:14–15)*

Most of us completely miss the point of Jesus' teachings on the
Reign (Kingdom) of God. Many of us Christians think the Reign of
God is an otherworldly heaven that Jesus was trying to help people
reach. It isn't and he wasn't. Jesus lived in the Roman Empire and
his people were oppressed. Life in the Empire was good if you were
a Roman citizen and were willing to follow the Roman religion,
which included a whole pantheon of gods. Romans would conquer
peoples and then add their gods to this pantheon. This didn't work
for first-century Jews. They could not worship the pantheon of gods
because they were strict monotheists. Rome touted a great "peace"
called the *Pax Romana*. The Roman method for establishing peace
was through conquest—so it was hardly peace! Jesus insisted on
peace not through conquest, but through justice.[1]

Understanding this context is central to understanding why
Jesus' primary message was about working for a peace that is only
possible when there is a true justice for all people. When Jesus
spoke about the Reign of God, he was speaking about a radical
vision that he had for the future in which everyone had enough,
all were welcome, and ultimate loyalty was not to the emperor (or
to Donald Trump or any other political leader), but to God. Can
you see how that got him into trouble? Moreover, he declared that
the Reign of God is "among you,"[2] meaning that the establishment
of peace and justice on this Earth cannot wait, we must create
it right now. It was this declaration that got Jesus crucified for
insurrection—especially since Jesus' followers were proclaiming
that he was the Messiah, who was supposed to be a warrior-king
who would lead a violent revolution to overthrow the government
and reestablish a self-ruled kingdom of Israel. Jesus defied

[1] Marcus Borg and John Dominic Crossan, *The First Christmas: What
the Gospels Really Teach about Jesus's Birth* (New York: HarperOne, 2007)
192.
[2] Luke 17:21.

messianic expectations by talking about a nonviolent revolution of the heart in which there was a metaphorical "kingdom" (a just society) and where God reigned supreme as the ruler of our hearts, no matter what society we live in.

You can see how the Romans might not have liked these teachings. The Romans wouldn't have cared if Jesus were simply teaching people how to be kind to each other. The Romans wouldn't have cared if Jesus were focused on reaching the sweet bye-and-bye somewhere in the sky. The Romans wouldn't have cared if he had really taught about obeying authority (more on that in Week 27). The Romans cared because they thought that Judeans would revolt against Rome. Crucifixion was used exclusively as a public form of execution for people who were insurrectionists.[3] It was a public display of force and authority.[4] The lesson for us is that as Christians, we are always citizens of the Kingdom of God first and of our country second. God's Kingdom knows no borders, it isn't limited by national-origin, it embraces all ethnicities, and it calls on us to continue to work for peace and justice, no matter in which country with human-created borders we find ourselves living. May it be so.

QUESTIONS

- What do you think about the concept of establishing peace through the presence of justice in our society?

- What are some of the issues facing our society that might be eased by more social justice?

- What would it mean for you to be more loyal to God than to country?

- Where does being loyal to your country make it hard to be loyal to the ideals of Jesus?

---

[3] Marcus Borg and John Dominic Crossan, *The Last Week: What the Gospels Really Teach about Jesus's Final Days in Jerusalem* (New York: HarperOne, 2006), 28.

[4] The Jewish leaders did not kill Jesus, despite the accounts in the gospels. If they had sentenced him to death, they could have done so on their own authority and wouldn't have needed the Romans. The penalty would have been death by stoning.

- What would it be like to consider yourself a citizen of the Reign (Kingdom) of God?

Spiritual Practice

Nationalism entails blind loyalty to a country or its leader and is incredibly dangerous. Patriotism is a sense of pride in one's country while retaining the ability to be critical of it. A Christian can be a patriot, but not a nationalist. Spend some time thinking about how you see the intersection of religion and politics. The First Amendment to the Constitution reads, "Congress shall make no law respecting an establishment of religion, or prohibiting the free exercise thereof; or abridging the freedom of speech, or of the press; or the right of the people peaceably to assemble, and to petition the Government for a redress of grievances."[5] Pay particular attention to the portion about religion (called the Establishment and Free Exercise Clauses). How do you interpret this amendment? Spend some time writing down your reflections.

Video Reflection

Don't forget to scan the QR Code on the cover of this book for more on this topic and a mid-week spiritual practice.

---

[5] Constitution of the United States of America, https://constitution. congress.gov/constitution/amendment-1/.

Week 26 – Reign of God: Understanding Terms

Now when the centurion who stood facing him saw that in this way he breathed his last, he said, "Truly this man was God's Son!" (Mark 15:39)

Then he began to teach them that the Son of Man must undergo great suffering and be rejected by the elders, the chief priests, and the scribes and be killed and after three days rise again. (Mark 8:31)

The gospels call Jesus both the Son of God and the Son of Man. Often, Christians take this to mean that he is both fully divine and fully human. However, that interpretation is read through the lens of the ecumenical councils in the fourth century that decided that Jesus was both fully divine and fully human. Early Jesus followers were divided about this issue. Let me give you a sampling of some early Christian views on Jesus. You'll recall from earlier that Jewish Christian Adoptionists believed that Jesus was fully human, but that God adopted him as a son at his baptism. Marcionite Christians, on the other hand, believed that Jesus was completely divine and only existed on this Earth as a spirit, a sort of phantasm, and consequently that he only appeared to suffer on the cross.[6] I'm not advocating either of those beliefs, I simply think it's interesting that modern Christians assume that early Jesus-followers were all in agreement about his teachings, and that the division that resulted happened much later. Not true! Jesus' message was so radical that people have been trying to make sense of it for two thousand years.

Part of the confusion on our part comes from a lack of understanding of important terms. The term "Son of God" was a title that was often used in the ancient world, especially for leaders who were claiming authority over others. In fact, the Roman Emperor was called the "Son of God." Simply put, when Jesus' followers called Jesus the Son of God, they were saying that Jesus, not Caesar, is the one with a special relationship to God. "Son

---

[6] Ehrman, *The New Testament: A Historical Introduction to the Early Christian Writings*, 3–5.

of Man" can simply mean a human, but more importantly, it was a messianic title. When Jesus' followers claimed that he was the Son of Man, they were saying that they were loyal to the Reign of God and not to Rome. When we read the gospels, we need to have this historical understanding if we really want to comprehend what was so significant about Jesus' ministry and why he ended up on the cross.[7]

When we confess Jesus as the Son of God and as the Son of Man in the twenty-first century, we are making similar confessions as those early followers. We are saying that for us, Jesus is the one with the special relationship to God; Jesus is the one who is our best teacher about how we live, and we are loyal to him over any other human being. Christians who have compromised their integrity to support Donald Trump are a perfect example of loyalty to a person over the ideals of Jesus. When we confess that Jesus is the Son of Man, we are saying that we claim him as the Messiah who taught us about a different kind of social system where we would create a just social order with ultimate loyalty to our God who calls us to see the divinity within every person. That is the Jesus that we should all follow. May it be so. Amen.

QUESTIONS

- Who is Jesus to you?
- What is your Christology (how divine do you think Jesus is)?
- What is Jesus' relationship to God?
- How do you understand Jesus' relationship to government?
- How do you feel about calling Jesus the "Messiah" or "Christ"? What does that mean to you?

---

[7] Marcus Borg, "Christians in an Age of Empire, Then and Now," The Marcus Borg Foundation, May 17, 2008, https://marcusjborg.org/videos/christians-in-an-age-of-empire-then-and-now/.

Spiritual Practice

Take a few moments and sit down with a piece of paper or a journal. Think about ways that you've seen religion and politics tied together. What has made you uncomfortable? In what ways do you think they belong together? As you reflect, write down your thoughts. Maybe even draw a picture.

Video Reflection

Don't forget to scan the QR Code on the cover of this book for more on this topic and a mid-week spiritual practice.

Week 27 – Reign of God:
Our Relationship to Government

*"Bring me a denarius and let me see it." And they brought one.
Then he said to them, "Whose head is this, and whose title?"
They answered, "The emperor's." Jesus said to them, "Give to
the emperor the things that are the emperor's, and to God the
things that are God's." And they were utterly amazed at him.
(Mark 12:15b–17)[8]*

One factor that complicates following Jesus is that he rarely
explained his teachings. This frustrating practice left and currently
leaves his followers with a great deal of interpretive freedom. This
is further complicated by many people now reading these teachings
with limited understanding of the socio-historical context in
which they were spoken. This week's centering scripture is one
of the most misunderstood texts in the Bible because people read
it through the lens of their own cultural experience. One of the
most common interpretations is that this teaching justifies the
separation of church and state. I can say with one hundred percent
certainty that is an incorrect interpretation because the very idea
that church and state should be separate (imperative as it is!) is a
product of the Enlightenment period and is anachronistic to apply
it to first-century teaching. Some people also say that this week's
scripture is about respecting the emperor's authority, but that is
completely inconsistent with the rest of Jesus' teachings.

This text comes from a question about whether Judeans should pay
taxes. Taxes were extremely unpopular, because Judeans were an
oppressed people, and they did not like paying authorities for their
oppression. Further, tax collectors often skimmed money from
those taxes for themselves, which is why they were unpopular
throughout the gospels. The text says that this question was an
attempt to trap Jesus. This is an apt description because there was
no great answer. If he said that they should pay taxes, it would
breed animosity from his followers who were anti-imperial (as
were most Judeans who weren't in power). If he said they should
not pay taxes, this was a punishable act of insurrection. Instead

---

[8] *New Revised Standard Version.*

of responding unequivocally, Jesus gave an answer marked by his typical ambiguity while also making it clear to those around him what he meant.

To understand this lesson, you must know what's on the coin in question. Most scholars believe that the coin was a denarius that would have had an image of the emperor on it with an inscription containing a claim to the emperor's divinity.[9] Picture this coin in your mind's eye as you think about the narrative in question. Jesus is asked if it's lawful to pay taxes. Jesus shows them the coin with the emperor's head with the claim that Caesar is the son of god. Then he says that they ought to give to Caesar what is Caesar's and to God whatever is God's. Here, he is asking people to choose for themselves. Who is your God? Is it Caesar? Is it the one true God? Whom are you following? Jesus' question to us is the same. Where are our priorities? Who is our God? May we choose the God of love and liberation. May it be so. Amen.

QUESTIONS

- Does it change a scripture when it is read from a position of power rather than oppression?

- Romans made Caesar their god. What or whom do we make into our gods in the twenty-first century?

- What are some ways our country acts as a modern empire?

- How can Jesus' teachings about empire inform how we relate to the government?

- What are ways in which we are loyal to the values of our country over the values of God?

Spiritual Practice

If you are able, go to a place you associate with the government, perhaps your local city hall. If possible, go to a meeting. While there, think about the decisions that are being made. How do those decisions align with your values? Who is being excluded?

---

[9] Borg and Crossan, *The Last Week: What the Gospels Really Teach about Jesus's Final Days in Jerusalem*, 64.

What groups are and aren't represented? If you can, pray outside the building for love and justice to prevail. If needed, protests and demonstrations can also be forms of prayer and are deeply spiritual practices!

Video Reflection

Don't forget to scan the QR Code on the cover of this book for more on this topic and a mid-week spiritual practice.

Week 28 - Reign of God: Exorcizing Empire

....

Jesus then asked him, 'What is your name?' He said, 'Legion,'
for many demons had entered him. They begged him not to
order them to go back into the abyss. Now there on the hillside
a large herd of swine was feeding, and the demons begged
Jesus to let them enter these. So he gave them permission. Then
the demons came out of the man and entered the swine, and
the herd stampeded down the steep bank into the lake and was
drowned. (Luke 8:30–33)

Let's get something straight: there is evil in the world. However, demonic and magical beings do not cause it, and this scripture is perfect proof. I've already mentioned in the section on mental health that exorcisms are used in the gospels to try to explain issues in society. In this case, Jesus comes across a man who is possessed not by a single demon but by many demons. Jesus always asks the demon its name because in the ancient world knowing the name of the demon gave you control over it. (There's a real lesson here about how being able to name our demons/struggles is the first step in being able to confront them.) When the demons answer, they give their name as "legion."

In this Roman-occupied land, a legion only meant one thing: it described the largest regiment of the Roman army. If we were reading this story in Judea two thousand years ago, we would instantly have recognized what this story was about.[10] It wasn't a literal story about a man who was possessed by a demon from hell, but a metaphor for how Judea (the man) was being overtaken (possessed) by the Roman army (legion). When Jesus drives out the demon, the narrative acts as a parable of sorts about the desire of the Judeans to drive the Romans out of their land. As you know, since Jesus' followers confessed Jesus as the Messiah, driving out the Romans is exactly what they were hoping he would do.[11] As if this weren't clear enough, the symbol of the legion that Rome

---

[10] J. Nelson Kraybill, "To Hell with the Pigs!," *Anabaptist World* (blog), August 17, 2015, https://anabaptistworld.org/to-hell-with-the-pigs/#:~:text=That%20was%20the%20term%20for,occupying%20force%20was%20%E2%80%94%20a%20pig!.

[11] Ehrman, *The New Testament*, 77–78.

had used to subdue Judea was a pig![12] This is why Jesus exorcizes the demons into pigs and they then run off a cliff to their doom.

Doesn't knowing the socio-historical context completely reframe how we view this weird scripture? It's no longer about evil spirits taking possession of a human body, but rather about an empire taking possession of a land that was not their own, and about people's desire for autonomy and freedom from Roman oppression. Those of us who live in the United States must come to terms with the fact that the United States has acted and continues to act as an empire in many ways. The US was built on the graves of indigenous peoples, and the backs of black slaves and, despite rhetoric to the contrary, it continues to oppress minorities within its borders. The US has inserted ourselves into the political affairs of other nations often acting as judge, jury, and executioner with little concern for how those actions affect the most vulnerable people in those societies. We still treat Puerto Rico as a colony of the US by denying these US citizens voting representation in Congress. Perhaps Jesus' teachings on confronting empire are not as foreign as they initially seem! May Jesus inspire us to advocate for those who are most marginalized in society. May it be so. Amen.

QUESTIONS

- What do you think about the idea that most evil in the world is not the work of a supernatural force, but the result of human behavior?

- Are there other instances that come to mind with the US acting as an empire?

- If we think about Jesus' exorcisms as commenting on social issues of the day, does that change how we think about Jesus?

- Are there any demons in your own life that you need to name? In your community? In society?

- If there are demons to name, what's the first step in confronting them?

---

[12] Kraybill, "To Hell with the Pigs!"

Spiritual Practice

Take a few moments and think about how the US has acted as an empire in the past. Make a list. Now think about how we Americans continue to act as an empire. Write those down, as well. Take a few moments to reflect on what our faith tells us about these actions and how we should respond.

Video Reflection

Don't forget to scan the QR Code on the cover of this book for more on this topic and a mid-week spiritual practice.

QUESTIONING

Week 29 – Questioning: Living with the Questions

*When he was alone, those who were around him along with
the twelve asked him about the parables. And he said to them,
"To you has been given the secret of the kingdom of God, but
for those outside everything comes in parables, in order that
'they may indeed look, but not perceive, and may indeed listen,
but not understand; so that they may not turn again and be
forgiven.'" (Mark 4:10–12)*

When reading this verse in the past, it has always struck me as a bit
Gnostic. Gnostic Christians believe(d) that there is an inner spark
of divinity in each person that can only be obtained by attaining
the proper *gnosis* or knowledge. This knowledge is like a key to
unlocking one's spiritual self. For Gnostics, humans were (are)
inherently spiritual beings who are trapped in the physical world.
Having Jesus' teachings was not enough; people also needed the
correct understanding of the teachings for their spiritual nature
to be released. Once their inner spark was set free, they could be
unified with God.[1] We typically think that Jesus taught in parables
to help people gain greater insight and understanding, so it's a bit
jarring to come across this verse in Mark that seems to indicate
that Jesus was using parables to confuse people, not to help them.

I believe there is some element of Gnostic tradition filtering into
the passage. Jesus is also commenting on people's willingness to
engage with the lesson rather than accepting it without thinking.
Jesus' disciples had dropped everything in their lives to follow a
nomadic rabbi who depended entirely upon the hospitality of
others. They listened to him teach day after day, discussed his
teachings, and wrestled with what that instruction meant for
their lives. Still, the gospels portray them as people who didn't
understand what Jesus was talking about much of the time.

This week's centering scripture is found within the Parable of the
Sower. Jesus spoke the parable without explanation to a crowd,
but when the disciples were alone with him, they had questions.
Not just about this specific parable, but about "the parables." Jesus

---

[1] Ehrman, *The New Testament*, 6.

tells them that they have "been given the secret to the kingdom of God" and explains what the parable means. Why have they been given the knowledge? It seems that it was because they were willing to ask the questions. In fact, when people ask Jesus questions, he always replies, even if he responds with a parable or another question. Clearly, Jesus deeply appreciated questions.

Sometimes we get so focused on finding the right answer that we forget about the power of questions. The Church has been guilty of wanting to provide people with delineated answers to questions that are ultimately not *truly* answers, but theological guesses. Human beings have striven to create a coherent theology since the beginning of time. Ultimately the best that we can do is acknowledge that God is ineffable. It is through asking hard questions and allowing ourselves to be uncomfortable with not knowing the answers that we begin to grow spiritually. In Progressive Christianity, we recognize that ultimately the questions are more important than the answers. Whatever conclusions we reach are ultimately unprovable, no matter how strongly we believe them. But asking the questions allows us to go beyond dichotomous thinking and allows us the room to grow. It also helps us to make space for the interpretations that others bring to the conversation. May it be so. Amen.

QUESTIONS

- What is currently your biggest faith question?

- When have there been times in your spiritual journey when you've changed your mind about a theological issue?

- Are there biblical passages (or even entire books of the Bible...here's looking at you, Revelation) that you struggle to understand?

- How do you respond to someone with a different theological interpretation than you?

- Which aspects of your theology are you unwilling to question?

Spiritual Practice

For this section, we will engage in an ancient Christian spiritual practice called *lectio divina*, or divine reading. There are several different ways to engage in this practice, and there is no wrong way to do it. Typically, though, there are four movements: *lectio* (reading), *meditatio* (meditation or reflection), *oratio* (prayer), and *contemplatio* (contemplation). This week, read Mark 4:1–9 (the Parable of the Sower) or another passage of your choice. First, read the passage to yourself, have someone read it to you, or listen to it on an app. Don't engage with the passage much; just listen to the words, sit with the passage for a few moments, and notice if anything stands out to you. Second, reread the passage and discern what you think it means for you. Reflect on the passage. Are there lines or words that you've never thought about much before now, things that you hadn't noticed before? Third, reread the passage and end by praying in whatever manner you find comfortable about what you've discovered during your first two movements of lectio. Fourth, read the passage a final time and contemplate what you've learned, perhaps by journaling or making a note on your phone so that you don't forget the insights you've gained.

Video Reflection

Don't forget to scan the QR Code on the cover of this book for more on this topic and a mid-week spiritual practice.

Week 30 – Questioning: Searching for God

For we know only in part, and we prophesy only in part; but when the complete comes, the partial will come to an end. When I was a child, I spoke like a child, I thought like a child, I reasoned like a child; when I became an adult, I put an end to childish ways. For now we see in a mirror, dimly, but then we will see face to face. Now I know only in part; then I will know fully, even as I have been fully known. (1 Corinthians 13:9–12)[2]

Even if it is often misunderstood, 1 Corinthians 13 is one of the most beloved chapters in the entire Bible. "Love is patient, love is kind" are words we frequently hear at weddings applied to romantic love (*eros* in Greek). But here Paul is talking about neighborly love (*agape* in Greek). Paul spends much of this letter to the Corinthians talking about how they have failed to live up to the ideals of what it means to be a community. In the thirteenth chapter, he helps them to realize how they must treat each other if they are going to survive as a community. The chapter ends with a description of how he suggests viewing God. Paul is frequently arrogant about his beliefs, but here we get the best of Paul as he suggests humility with how we approach our knowledge of the sacred.

Many Christians want to approach faith as if it were a static goal to be attained, a constant pursuit for the right answers. Paul suggests otherwise, indicating that as we grow in age and, hopefully, wisdom, our faith grows and changes. In his book *Meeting Jesus Again for the First Time*, Marcus Borg suggests there are three phases of faith. The first is pre-critical naiveté, the phase in which we accept whatever we are taught because someone we respect has told us it's important to believe it. Think of a child accepting the seven-day creation myth as reality because a parent told them it's true. The child trusts the parent and blindly believes what they are told. The second phase is critical thinking. Here, we begin to question what we have been taught. For instance, we might question the seven-day creation story when we learn about evolution in science class. We recognize that both cannot be

---

[2] *New Revised Standard Version.*

factually accurate and must decide which we will believe. The final phase (one at which not everyone arrives) is post-critical naiveté and describes how we reconcile the two realities by realizing that a story can be true without being factual. In the case of the creation story, it tells us about God's love for all the Earth without detailing historically how the universe came into being.[3]

Despite Paul's apparent confidence in all matters theological, he ultimately recognized that even our best attempts to understand the divine mystery give us only a glimpse of the truth. God is beyond our understanding. That doesn't mean we shouldn't try to understand how the sacred connects us. It does mean that throughout human history all the theologies and philosophies that have been developed ultimately fall short of the reality that is both real and unknowable. Paul puts it beautifully when he says, "For now we see in a mirror, dimly." I picture an old mirror, worn, where the reflection is obscured by age and no matter how much we strain to see, the reflection is never clear. But Paul has hope that one day we will understand; that one day we will be united with God and have rest in the knowledge of God's unconditional love. He also asserts that even if we don't fully know God, we are already fully known by God. It's hard to imagine a more life-giving realization than the fact that God fully knows us and has claimed us as we are. May we rest in that knowledge, even if we don't yet fully understand what it means. May it be so. Amen.

QUESTIONS

- How did you see God as a child?

- Have there been points in your journey at which you let go of belief in God? When and why?

- How has your view of God changed over time?

- What is it about God that you're wrestling with right now?

- What is it that you long to know about God?

---

[3] Marcus Borg, *Meeting Jesus Again for the First Time: The Historical Jesus & The Heart Of Contemporary Faith* (San Francisco: HarperSanFrancisco, 1994), 6–17.

Spiritual Practice

This week, we will continue the *lectio divina* exercise following the same pattern as before. This week, read 1 Corinthians 13 in its entirety. First, read the passage to yourself, have someone read it to you, or listen to it on an app. Don't engage with the passage much, just listen to the words, sit with the passage for a few moments and notice if anything stands out to you. Second, reread the passage and discern what you think it means for you. In short, reflect on the passage. Are there words or phrases you'd never thought about much before, things that you hadn't noticed? Third, reread the passage and end by praying about what you've discovered during your first two movements of *lectio*. Fourth, read the passage one final time and contemplate what you've learned, perhaps by journaling or making a note on your phone so that you don't forget the insights you've gained.

Video Reflection

Don't forget to scan the QR Code on the cover of this book for more on this topic and a mid-week spiritual practice.

Week 31 – Questioning: It's Worth the Effort

....

Ask, and it will be given to you; search, and you will find; knock, and the door will be opened for you. For everyone who asks receives, and everyone who searches finds, and for everyone who knocks, the door will be opened. Is there anyone among you who, if your child asked for bread, would give a stone? Or if the child asked for a fish, would give a snake? If you, then, who are evil, know how to give good gifts to your children, how much more will your Father in heaven give good things to those who ask him! (Matthew 7:7-11)

This week's centering scripture is from the Sermon on the Mount. The three chapters where we find this "sermon" in Matthew's Gospel are likely my favorite in the entire Bible. Here, Jesus reinterprets what the law that his people are following means. Most Bibles have headings and divide the teachings into sections, but it's really a collection of teachings and parables, many without clear explanation...which are my favorite kind! When we read through the Bible, we often don't realize that the explanations that come from Jesus in the text were almost certainly placed in Jesus' mouth by the author to explain the teachings to the communities for which the gospels were written. It seems clear that Jesus typically didn't explain his teachings but left them open to interpretation. Most scholars think that many of Jesus' sayings in the Gospels of Matthew and Luke came from a source called "Q" from the German word *Quelle* or "source."[4] This source likely didn't contain explanations, just the sayings.

Gnostic gospels are often looked down upon as ahistorical and ultimately irrelevant, but I don't think either of those perceptions is true. The scholarly consensus is that most of these noncanonical texts[5] were written later than those in the Bible.[6] But that doesn't mean they don't matter! Although they may not show us what Jesus taught, they provide valuable insight into what early Christian communities believed. The one exception is the Gospel of Thomas,

---

[4] Ehrman, *The New Testament*, 84.
[5] Noncanonical texts include gospels that are not in the Bible.
[6] Ehrman, *The New Testament*, 196.

which is a collection of sayings like Q, and I side with scholars—like those in the Jesus Seminar—who believe that it was written in the first century and contains authentic teachings of Jesus.[7] The Gospel of Thomas provides teachings with little to no explanation, proving that there was a great deal of diversity in early communities about the proper interpretation of Jesus' teachings. Further, some teachings are downright odd. I think this shows us that early Jesus followers didn't always understand his teachings, and there was a lot left open to interpretation.

Jesus says, "Everyone who asks receives, and everyone who searches finds, and for everyone who knocks, the door will be opened." When Jesus tells us that we will receive, find, and discover an open door, you'll notice that none of that happens without effort. To receive, you must ask. To find what you're looking for, you must go on the journey and seek it. If you want someone inside to open the door, the only way they'll know you're there, is if you knock! Faith is like that. It's not passive. Faith is a willingness to *ask* hard questions, *search* for truth, and *knock* on the door of new ideas for fresh understandings to open our minds. May it be so. Amen.

QUESTIONS

- What question do you wish would simply be answered?

- How does it change your faith to know that many of the interpretations of Jesus' teachings were likely given by the authors of the text, not Jesus?

- Have you ever read any non-canonical gospels? If so, what was your impression? If not, are you open to reading them?

- What do you think about the idea of a vending machine God?

- How do you understand the purpose of prayer?

---

[7] Robert W. Funk, Roy W. Hoover, and The Jesus Seminar, *The Five Gospels: The Search for the Authentic Words of Jesus* (San Francisco: Harper-SanFrancisco, 1993), 18.

Spiritual Practice

This week, we will continue the *lectio divina* exercise following the same pattern as before. This week, read all or part of Matthew 7. First, read the passage to yourself, have someone read it to you, or listen to it on an app. Don't engage with the passage much; just listen to the words, sit with the passage for a few moments and notice if anything stands out to you. Second, reread the passage and discern what you think it means for you. In short, reflect on the passage. Are there lines that you've never really considered deeply until now? Things that you hadn't noticed before? Third, reread the passage and end by praying about what you've discovered during your first two movements of lectio. Fourth, read the passage a final time and contemplate what you've learned, perhaps by journaling or making a note on your phone, so you don't forget the insights that you've gained.

Video Reflection

Don't forget to scan the QR Code on the cover of this book for more on this topic and a mid-week spiritual practice.

Week 32 – Questioning: Even Jesus Had Questions

....

When it was noon, darkness came over the whole land until three in the afternoon. At three o'clock Jesus cried out with a loud voice, "Eloi, Eloi, lema sabachthani?" which means, "My God, my God, why have you forsaken me?" (Mark 15:33–34)

No matter where you are on the theological spectrum, the crucifixion is a seminal event of the Christian faith. We tend to think of a unified passion narrative but the truth is that each of the gospels portrays the events differently, depending on the theological and political points that the author is making. The various authors approach Jesus' last words in different ways too. Many traditions observe seven last sayings services on Good Friday at which each of the seven sayings is explored. Through such an exploration, we compile a narrative that frankly takes away from the richness of each of the individual stories. In Mark and Matthew, Jesus ends his life by asking a question: "My God, my God, why have you forsaken me?" Mark's is the gospel in which Jesus seems the most human. In this moment of anguish, a very human Jesus cries out to God hoping for an answer. This phrase is from Psalm 22. It shouldn't surprise us that this rabbi, who is dying for his beliefs, decides to quote scripture with his final breath. The Psalmist feels distant from God and longs to know God's presence, but ultimately understands that God is there, even if it doesn't feel like it. It's a prayer of sorts in the form of a question.

Mark is a fascinating gospel because the version that we have isn't what the author wrote. In Mark, Jesus is crucified, placed in a tomb, and the most ancient manuscripts end with Mark 16:8. Mary Magdalene, Mary the mother of James, and Salome have come on Sunday morning to anoint Jesus' body. When they arrive, they find an empty tomb and a young man in a white robe who tells them that Jesus is not there. The women run away scared and tell no one. End of the gospel. There was no explanation for the empty tomb. There were no resurrection appearances to the disciples. There was simply an empty tomb and fear. You can probably understand why a later editor decided to add the appearances of Jesus to his followers and an ascension into heaven! It may be an unpopular opinion, but I prefer the original version. We find a Jesus who speaks his final words to God in the form of a question. In fact, the gospel itself ends in a bit of a question. What exactly happened to Jesus? Where did he go? What are his followers to do now?

I appreciate each of the gospels that we have in the New Testament for different reasons, but the Gospel of Mark has my favorite ending by far. People often seek a faith that is merely a list of prescribed answers to our questions. Mark's gospel stands in stark opposition to such a philosophy. Jesus doesn't get an answer to his question on the cross. Mark doesn't give an answer to what happened to Jesus. The story of Jesus ends in a cliffhanger...but we get to answer it with our lives. Who is feeling "forsaken" or abandoned? How might we come alongside them? If we feel deserted ourselves, we can take comfort in knowing that *even Jesus* felt that way and wondered why. We also get to answer the question of the empty tomb. Where did Jesus go? Where is he now? *He's here.* Jesus shows up everywhere that we pursue justice, practice compassion, embrace forgiveness, and become radically inclusive. Our lives are the answer. I usually prefer the questions to the answers, but that's one answer that I can get behind. May it be so. Amen.

QUESTIONS

- What do you think of the original ending of Mark?

- When have you felt abandoned by someone? How about by God?

- How does your life answer the question of the empty tomb?

- Do you resonate more with the human portrayal of Jesus or the divine one?

- What do you make of the women running away scared in the Gospel of Mark?

Spiritual Practice

This week, we will continue the *lectio divina* exercise following the same pattern as before. This week, read all or part of Mark 16:1-8 (the original ending). First, read the passage to yourself, have someone read it to you, or listen to it on an app. Don't engage with the passage much, just listen to the words, sit with the passage for a few moments and notice if anything stands out to you. Second, reread the passage and discern what you think it means for you. In short, reflect on the passage. Are there lines in it that you'd never considered much before? Are there things that you haven't noticed before? Third, reread the passage and end by praying about what you've discovered during your first two movements of *lectio*. Fourth, read the passage once more and contemplate what you've learned, perhaps by journaling or making a note on your phone, so that you don't forget the insights that you've gained.

Video Reflection

Don't forget to scan the QR Code on the cover of this book for more on this topic and a mid-week spiritual practice.

FAITH IN SCIENCE

Week 33 – Faith in Science: The Heart of the Issue

....

On the sixth day God finished the work that he had done, and he rested on the seventh day from all the work that he had done. So God blessed the seventh day and hallowed it, because on it God rested from all the work that he had done in creation. These are the generations of the heavens and the earth when they were created. (Genesis 2:2–4)

When I was a freshman at a secular university, I took an Intro to Religion class. One day, a student raised his hand and asked the professor why we even bothered learning about religion, especially in college. "Don't you think that one day science will completely replace religion and we can be done with all of this nonsense?" he asked. This professor specialized in the intersection of psychology and religion. Without missing a beat, he said, "No. Because they ask fundamentally different questions. Science asks *how*. Religion asks *why*." The student's question was meant to poke fun at what he regarded as the superstitious nature of religion, but the professor's answer was profound for me. I always knew that science and religion weren't mutually exclusive, but I couldn't articulate why. Besides, such a stance was somewhat counter-intuitive in the small corner of the world in which I grew up, where you are either religious and believe in a literal interpretation of myth or you are an atheist and trust in science...I did grow up in rural Missouri after all! Clearly, we are all too often presented with a false dichotomy.

Science and religion shouldn't be pitted against each other. Rather than competing, they complete each other. They are two sides of the same coin; they are different ways of making sense of the world. Science is concerned with helping us to understand how the universe works, but it can never really answer the question of purpose: *Why* are we here? In the same way, religion asks existential questions, but can't explain the *how* of the universe, because it was never meant to do that, no matter how much some people try to convince us that it does. The opening pages of the Bible are a case in point. The first creation story describes God's creation of the Earth over seven days. Was the world created in seven days? No. The Earth was formed over billions of years and science has proved this. Young Earth Creationists who claim that the Earth is only a few thousand years old have completely checked their brains at the door and have decided to worship the Bible as an idol.

Why does the Bible portray the Earth as being created in seven days if it isn't reality? The story wasn't designed to be read as a science textbook: it's an etiology.[1] Ancient people didn't understand how the Earth came to be, but they recognized that there was a greater force than themselves at work in its formation. As a result, they told a beautiful story about each piece of the world being handcrafted by God, and they modeled the story after the days of the week. When we see the story in that light, it goes from being a fact-denying shackle to a liberating story about a God at work amid all things. When I think of God, I picture a force at work in our universe beyond description and understanding. The work of religion is about striving to understand that force. Quite frankly, that's also the work of science. Embracing a truth-seeking, fact-finding theology allows us to have faith in God and in science. May it be so. Amen.

QUESTIONS

- How do you understand the connection between faith and science?

- How has your view of science and religion changed over time?

- What scientific findings have challenged your faith?

- What scientific findings have nourished your faith?

- Why do you think our culture often sees science and religion as incompatible?

Spiritual Practice

All too often, we lose our sense of wonder. Being curious about the world is a deeply spiritual practice that can lead to moments

---

[1] A story designed to help make sense of the world and how it came to be the way that it is.

of complete awe. This week, try to find time to go outside in the evening, perhaps at night when you can see stars in the sky. If there's light pollution, notice how that affects your connection to the world around you. As you look at the sky, think about the stars and how you are looking into the past. Some of the stars' lights reach us in a few years or a few hundred years, but by the time it reaches us the light of other stars is millions of years old. Light from our nearest galaxy takes over two million years to reach us. There may be as many as two *trillion* galaxies in the universe.[2] Sit or stand in awe of the universe for a few moments. How do you feel?

Video Reflection

Don't forget to scan the QR Code on the cover of this book for more on this topic and a mid-week spiritual practice.

---

[2] NASA Hubble Mission Team, "New Horizons Spacecraft Answers Question: How Dark Is Space?," January 13, 2021, https://science.nasa.gov/missions/hubble/new-horizons-spacecraft-answers-question-how-dark-is-space/.

Week 34 – Faith in Science: Using our Minds

....

You shall love the Lord your God with all your heart and with all your soul and with all your mind and with all your strength. (Mark 12:30)

Versions of the Great Commandment are found in all three synoptic gospels and are each tied to the command to "love your neighbor as yourself." Jesus didn't invent the commandment; he's simply quoting from Deuteronomy. He was a rabbi after all! Do you ever find yourself struggling to get the wording of the first part of the quotation right? I do. Perhaps it's because none of the versions are quite the same. Deuteronomy cites it as "You shall love the Lord your God with all your heart and with all your soul and with all your might."[3] Matthew reports, "You shall love the Lord your God with all your heart and with all your soul and with all your mind."[4] Luke states, "You shall love the Lord your God with all your heart and with all your soul and with all your strength and with all your mind."[5] Mark's version is similar to Luke's, but places "mind" earlier in the order. The mind is not an afterthought in Mark as it appears in Matthew and Luke.

It's fascinating to me that Jesus takes the Great Commandment from the Hebrew Bible and adds "mind" to the essential ways that we are to love God. Loving God is not merely about passion or emotion, but also of thought and reason. Thinking is a Christian value. If we are going to love God with everything we have, then that must include our brains! Modern Christianity has become adept at denying facts in favor of a blind fundamentalist faith. People think that accepting that which is illogical somehow makes them better Christians. Quite frankly, nothing could be further from the truth. Checking our brains at the door of the church is antithetical to Jesus' teachings. God gave us brains for a reason, and we ought to use them! Refusing to interrogate the world in which we live falls short of the Great Commandment. If we believe that God is really at work in our universe, then why wouldn't we want

---

[3] Deuteronomy 6:5.
[4] Matthew 22:37.
[5] Luke 10:27.

to discover as much as we can about how this universe works? Or to put it another way: God is the universe. The universe is God. By learning about our physics, biology, geology, astronomy, chemistry, ecology, etc. we are really learning about God.

Part of the problem with the way religious folks tend to think is that we think of God as way too small. In fact, God is beyond our understanding. To cope with this reality, we often anthropomorphize God. There's nothing inherently wrong with visualizing God as a person to help us to relate to the cosmic reality. Thinking about the vastness of the universe can be both awe-inspiring and completely overwhelming. However, we must always recognize that the God we visualize in our mind's eye: the being to whom we speak in prayer, the one whom we hope is with us each day; exists as truly as do the laws of science that we discover in our natural world. It's not heretical to view God in this way; it embraces the reality that we know to be true. If more Christians embraced the notion that God was beyond definition and that science might help us to understand our ultimate reality, perhaps our minds might expand, and we could love God more fully. May it be so. Amen.

QUESTIONS

- Which version of the Great Commandment do you prefer? Why?

- What would it feel like to embrace the concept of the universe as God?

- If we embrace a more expansive notion of God, what does • Jesus' role become?

- When have there been times when new information has helped you to think about God differently?

- How could churches do a better job of integrating the findings of science into their theology?

Spiritual Practice

Go online and Google "recent scientific discoveries." Scroll and find an article from a reputable source that interests you. For instance, visit the websites of the Smithsonian, NASA, or Scientific American. Take time to read the article and digest the findings. Think about how the article relates to your faith.

Video Reflection

Don't forget to scan the QR Code on the cover of this book for more on this topic and a mid-week spiritual practice.

Week 35 – Faith in Science: Knowing Our Place

When I look at your heavens, the work of your fingers, the moon and the stars that you have established; what are humans that you are mindful of them, mortals that you care for them? Yet you have made them a little lower than God and crowned them with glory and honor. You have given them dominion over the works of your hands; you have put all things under their feet, all sheep and oxen, and also the beasts of the field, the birds of the air, and the fish of the sea, whatever passes along the paths of the seas. (Psalm 8:3–8)

As we go about our lives, it's incredibly easy to become hyper-focused on our own reality. Our next project at work, an upcoming assignment at school, a difficult family situation, or an arising health concern can seem like the most important things in the universe. One thing that science and religion both remind us about is how small we are in the grand scheme of things. That can snap things into perspective quickly. It can be both liberating to know that most of the mundane tasks we deal with daily are relatively small compared to the universe and incredibly humbling to know that our entire world (literally) is but a speck on the cosmic scale. In Psalm 8, the Psalmist has a moment of perspective in which he realizes that humans have it pretty good, all things considered. Yes, there are certainly struggles, but we have it better than the other creatures on the Earth. The Psalmist looks around with a sense of wonder and appreciates the beauty and intricacy of the world around them. You can almost visualize the Psalmist looking at something as small as a ladybug crawling along a leaf and saying, "Wow!" We get so used to life as usual that sometimes we forget to allow ourselves to be impressed that this world exists and is more intricate than we can fathom.

Turning to science helps us to gain an even deeper appreciation for all that allows this universe to be. Think of an atom, which is smaller than the human brain can truly fathom. For instance, a human hair is a *million* carbon atoms wide![6] What's more, we all know there are even smaller electrons, protons, and neutrons swirling inside those atoms. On the flip side, the universe is so inconceivably large that it has as many as 2 trillion galaxies and is 97 billion light years across and continues growing.[7] Now let's contextualize this. To assume that we have the one correct answer to the universe is so incredibly arrogant that it's difficult to articulate.

Science, though, can help us develop a more expansive and accurate theology. For instance, many scientists believe that all the matter that currently exists in the universe came into existence with the Big Bang. This means that once matter ceases being one thing, it becomes another. It also means that the matter that makes up our body will become something else when we die. I struggle with the idea of an eternal soul and an afterlife, but there is at least some truth in recognizing that our matter—some part of ourselves—will live on, will even be reincarnated. Science gives me hope that somehow human existence is beyond what we can understand. It helps keep me from the arrogance of thinking that I have it all figured out. May science continue to expand our minds. May it be so. Amen.

QUESTIONS

- When you think about the complexity necessary for our universe to exist, how does it make you feel?

- When you spend time looking at the world around you, thinking about your place in it, how does that influence your perspective?

- Do you believe in an afterlife? If so, what do you think it will be like?

- If we are all made of the same matter that was created at the Big Bang, does that make us all more connected?

---

[6] "Atom," in *Wikipedia*, n.d., https://en.wikipedia.org/wiki/Atom#:~:text=Atoms%20are%20extremely%20small%2C%20typically,see%20atoms%20with%20conventional%20microscopes.

[7] NASA Hubble Mission Team, "New Horizons Spacecraft Answers Question: How Dark Is Space?".

Spiritual Practice

If you're able, go outside and sit in nature. Pay attention to the smallest piece of nature that you can see. Perhaps it is a blade of grass, a leaf, or an insect. Think about your relation to that part of creation. After a few moments, look at the largest natural element around you. How do you relate to that part of creation? If you have access to a microscope and/or a telescope, spend some time thinking about the incredibly minute and the unfathomably large.

Video Reflection

Don't forget to scan the QR Code on the cover of this book for more on this topic and a mid-week spiritual practice.

Week 36 – Faith in Science: Science and Morality

....

Trust in the LORD with all your heart, and do not rely on your own insight. In all your ways acknowledge him, and he will make straight your paths. Do not be wise in your own eyes; fear the Lord and turn away from evil. (Proverbs 3:5–7)

Let's get one thing straight: it's not as if religion has always done the best job of being the moral voice. Christianity, in particular, has been used to justify some of the worst atrocities of human history, from the Crusades to slavery to the Holocaust to conversion therapy. However, when religion is at its best, it can be an important tool for helping us to navigate morally complex issues. A Pew Research study showed that many people see a clear distinction between the purposes of science and religion. They view religion as a moral guide on how to live a good life and science as a means of observing phenomena in the universe.[8]

Here's the issue: science isn't mere observation, is it? The research that is done and the discoveries that are made have real, lasting impacts on our lives and the world around us. Advancements in science and technology are happening at a breakneck pace, often without much forethought for how the findings will impact others. Many pharmaceutical companies have developed drugs that have the potential to save lives, yet mark them up at incredible rates for profit. They haven't merely discovered cures: they've patented, trademarked, marketed, and sold them to the few in the world who can afford them. The use and sophistication of artificial intelligence (AI) have skyrocketed in the past few years, and it's beginning to replace human beings in some industries. Likewise, AI has made it increasingly difficult to tell whether images and videos are real, moving us further into a post-truth society. We now can keep people alive for extended periods of time, even if they have little to no cognitive function. We *can* do a lot. The question becomes: What *should* we do? Surely faith has something to contribute to this conversation.

_____
[8] Pew Research Center, "On the Intersection of Science and Religion," August 26, 2020, https://www.pewresearch.org/religion/2020/08/26/on-the-intersection-of-science-and-religion/.

At its best, religion is supposed to be about guiding us through life's existential questions. Many people think the Bible is an answer book to life's questions. Viewing it that way trivializes its importance. How could a book with texts written millennia ago hope to provide the one right answer for any advancement made in the twenty-first century? For instance, study after study shows that while social media helps to connect us, the more time that we spend on it, the more depressed we are. How could the biblical authors even have fathomed the existence of social media, let alone the devices on which we access it? However, the Bible has examples of how people in different places, at different points in time navigated the issues of their day. We also discover plenty of times when people thought they had all the answers yet were humbled by the Divine. Turning to the Bible won't solve all our modern dilemmas, nor do I think there's one correct answer for most of the issues that science and technology raise. However, Jesus' teachings constantly remind us that we ought to have an ever-expanding view of God's love for us, and of our own call to love our neighbors. It seems that as we learn more about all that humanity can do, the religious message of what is best for human flourishing is likely going to be an important voice. May it be so. Amen.

QUESTIONS

- About which recent scientific or technological advances or inventions are you concerned? How does religion play a role in your answer?

- When have you rejected an advancement in technology because of your faith?

- When have you been faced with a moral dilemma brought about by science that your faith has helped you to navigate?

- What do you regard as being the biggest conversation between science and religion in the coming years?

- Should religion play a role in setting the moral tone of scientific research and advancement, or is it best for them to stay in separate spheres?

Spiritual Practice

Grab a sheet of paper or open your favorite electronic device. Take a few moments and think about an ethical issue raised by scientific advancement. Write it down. Think through the ethics of the issue. Write down how you are making sense of it. Try to let the teachings of Jesus influence your thoughts. Are there any scriptural texts that help you to make sense of the issue? Write them down. Are there texts that are unhelpful? Write those down, too.

Video Reflection

Don't forget to scan the QR Code on the cover of this book for more on this topic and a mid-week spiritual practice.

EMBRACING CHANGE

Week 37 – Embracing Change: Behaving, not Believing

···

> *Do not be conformed to this world, but be transformed by the*
> *renewing of your minds, so that you may discern what is the*
> *will of God—what is good and acceptable and perfect... "if your*
> *enemies are hungry, feed them; if they are thirsty, give them*
> *something to drink; for by doing this you will heap burning*
> *coals on their heads." Do not be overcome by evil, but overcome*
> *evil with good. (Romans 12:2, 20-21)[1]*

"We've always done it that way!" Maybe you've heard that refrain
resound in the hallowed halls of your faith community. Why is it
that we are so often afraid of change? It's understandable to fear
what we don't know, but it's not biblical. The Bible speaks quite a
bit about embracing God's change and not denying it. We get into
rhythms that, over time, feel comfortable, but breaking those
patterns can be an important spiritual practice, especially if we
find ourselves in a rut. Churches that continue to decline because
they won't break free from "tradition" deserve to die. Institutions
that ignore the writing on the wall fail because of their own doing.

Paul realized that following the teachings of Jesus was all about
transformation from the inside out; Jesus' ministry was about
personal and systemic change. He spoke about striving to let go
of negative thoughts about others, embracing forgiveness, and
letting the Reign of God dwell within us. By embracing these inner
forms of peace, he recognized that it would lead to an outward
transfiguration of the world through personal character. I do not
like to talk about Jesus as a savior, but embracing these ideals
can certainly be salvific! When we are at peace with ourselves,
it's easier to be at peace in the world. When we have modified
our behavior, it leads to a transformation of the world. This is
why Martin Luther King, Jr. believed so adamantly in nonviolent
resistance. He recognized that true systemic change begins
inwardly (by fully embracing nonviolence), and it leads to outward
action (through systemic change).

---

[1] *New Revised Standard Version.*

In this week's centering scripture, the renewal that Paul is discussing is an entirely different way of thinking. It involves a full commitment to Jesus' teachings in a way that transforms how we feel, think, and act. Much of American Christianity doesn't truly seem to be committed to these completely life-altering ideals. To follow Jesus, we can't simply say that we've had a moment of salvation in which we confessed Christ as "Our Lord and Savior," and call it good. Following Jesus ultimately isn't really about belief but about behavior. God cares more about how we behave than what we believe. Religion should never be confined to the four walls of a Church building or mere worship on a Sunday morning. If that's all that our faith is, then it's right and good for organized religion to disappear completely. Rather than filling pews, we need to fill the world with God's peace and justice. By doing so, we might just discover an incredible transformation ourselves. May it be so. Amen.

QUESTIONS

- When have you had a change in belief that has led to a change in your life?
- What spiritual practices have been transformative for you?
- Are there changes that would be helpful for you to make in your life right now?
- How have your beliefs about God or religion changed over time?
- What changes might lead to more inward peace for you?

Spiritual Practice

Each week this section about our spiritual practice will involve trying something new. This week, think about a way to help others that you've never tried before and commit to doing it this week. Perhaps you could volunteer at a food bank. Perhaps you could make a conversation with someone who is unhoused and let them know that you see them. Is there a friend who needs a ride to a doctor's appointment whom you could drive? If you feel so inclined, write down what it felt like to help someone in a different way than you've done before.

Video Reflection

Don't forget to scan the QR Code on the cover of this book for more on this topic and a mid-week spiritual practice.

Week 38 – Embracing Change: Making All Things New

*Then I saw a new heaven and a new earth for the first heaven
and the first earth had passed away, and the sea was no
more..."See, I am making all things new..." (Revelation 21:1, 5)*

The Book of Revelation isn't about end times: it's about the Roman
Empire's persecution of early Jesus followers. It's written in coded
language because that was the only way to criticize the most
powerful empire on Earth without being put to death. John, who
wrote Revelation, casts a vision for a future when things will be
different for his people. In this idyllic future, God dwells among
all mortals, and everyone is a part of God's family. It is a time
when God "will wipe every tear from their eyes" and "mourning
and crying and pain will be no more" (v. 4). In a world filled with
violence, oppression, and persecution, John's optimism for the
future shines through this oft-misunderstood text. Read in this
context, Revelation goes from being a creepy book at the end of the
Bible filled with terrifying imagery to an imaginative visualization
of a hopeful future amid a world that felt like it was going to end.
I love the Book of Revelation because it's an incredibly honest
book about how messed up the world can be, but it holds that
a transfiguration of the world to look more like God's Reign is
possible.

The world is constantly changing, and our lives are not the
same from moment to moment. The only moment that we are
guaranteed is the very moment that we are in. God is constantly
making all things new...including us. In the West, self-identity is
extremely important. Our culture and society encourage us to "find
ourselves" and then to "become who we're meant to be." Identity
needn't be stagnant. Who we are is dynamic. The reality is that
while we have certain traits and characteristics, we are constantly
being formed and re-formed by our relationships and experiences.
Who we are is not predetermined and it's not set in stone. We can
decide who we want to be and work towards being that person. I
believe that God is like a force that is always present in our lives
and that if we are attuned to the Sacred in the universe and allow
it to flow through us, it can also transform us. This means that at

any time we can be a new creation. This is particularly true if we need to make changes.

Too often, we cannot address the issues that we need to deal with because we refuse to acknowledge them. Are there places in our lives where we are unhappy? By recognizing those spaces and naming them, we have taken the first step to address any necessary alterations. The same is true whenever we are thinking about the injustices in the world. Simply pretending that they don't exist doesn't do anyone any favors. It makes us a part of the problem. Can we acknowledge that climate change is real and that we need to do something about it? Are we willing to admit blind spots in our knowledge about the spectrum of gender identities or sexual orientations that cause us to say harmful things to our siblings in Christ? Do we have the courage to go beyond "colorblindness" so that we might do something about the exploitation of black and brown people? A consistent message in the Bible is that God desires a "new heaven and a new earth," but it's a misinterpretation of scripture to think that there's going to be some cataclysmic event in which God will do all the work for us. To think so is a cop-out. Scripture makes it clear: God doesn't merely want a transformed world; God wants *us to transform* the world. May it be so. Amen.

QUESTIONS

- How have you changed over time?
- Which of your traits always stay the same?
- What change in your life have you been avoiding?
- What's something in the world that society avoids talking about?
- To create "a new heaven and a new earth," what should we change first?

Spiritual Practice

Each week, the spiritual practice described in this section will involve trying something new. This week, try something you've never done before that feels exciting. Is there a new restaurant with interesting food nearby? Have you always wanted to learn to surf? Would it be freeing to take a hike in a new spot? Whatever it is, create space for yourself this week. If you feel so inclined, write down what the experience was like for you.

Video Reflection

Don't forget to scan the QR Code on the cover of this book for more on this topic and a mid-week spiritual practice.

Week 39 – Embracing Change: God's Constant Presence

But this I call to mind, and therefore I have hope: The steadfast love of [God] never ceases, [God's] mercies never come to an end; they are new every morning; great is your faithfulness. (Lamentations 3:21-23)

God never promises that life won't be difficult. God never promises that we won't suffer. God never promises that everything will work out for us in the end. What God does promise is to be with us no matter what we're going through. God promises never to abandon us, even if we aren't aware of God's presence. This may seem like a meager notion of the Divine, but it's stronger than believing that God controls everything in our lives. If we truly believe that God is *in control* of our lives, then we must deal with some incredibly difficult theological questions. Questions like: Why would God allow horrific diseases, extreme poverty, gun violence, and war? Why would God make some people's lives easier than others? Why would God allow the world to continue in the state it's in? If all the evil and suffering in the world are a part of God's plan—even if the end goal is ultimate peace—that's not a god that I have any interest in worshiping. Belief in a God who is all-knowing and all-powerful brings a ton of ethical questions to which there are no satisfying answers.

The Book of Lamentations is a collection of poems that lament the destruction of Jerusalem by the Babylonians in 586 BCE, which resulted in the leveling of the Temple and the exile of the leaders to Babylon. To say that this destruction was devastating is an understatement. The ancient Israelites believed that God literally dwelt within the "Holy of Holies," the inner sanctum of the Temple. God was, of course, thought to be everywhere, but God dwelt particularly in that holy ground. When the Temple was gone, it felt very much as if God had not only abandoned the ancient Israelites but had been defeated. It is in mourning what has been lost that the verses in Lamentations 3 are written. Even in times of great despair, the steadfast love of God never ceases, because God is faithful. Over and over in scripture, we receive that promise. God has not been defeated. God has not and will not abandon us. To borrow a phrase from Paul, "Love Never Ends."

We tend to fear change because that which is unknown can feel terrifying. This can be true even if we are on the precipice of something wonderful. A sense of comfort and stability can ground us, but it can also be debilitating if it keeps us from growing. I find it incredibly comforting that the various authors of the Bible writing in differing times and places consistently described a similar experience of the Divine: God is *always* with us. Some of these authors lived during times of immense suffering, but the knowledge of God's consistent companionship offered them a sense of hope. No matter whether we understand God as a being, a force, the love that exists around us, or simply the great mystery of the universe, it makes a difference knowing that we are loved and that we are not alone. May that realization ground us and bolster us with the courage to embrace newness when it comes our way, even if we'd rather everything stay the same. May it be so. Amen.

QUESTIONS

- Recall a time when something changed for you when you truly wanted everything to stay the same. How did you deal with the unexpected or undesired change?

- How have you experienced God's presence during such times of change?

- When have you noticed an absence of God's presence?

- What role do you think God plays in our lives?

Spiritual Practice

Each week, this section on spiritual practice involves trying something new. This week try to read through a biblical text with which you have spent little time. If you haven't read Lamentations, maybe that's a good place to start. As you read, think about how you see the author striving to make sense of their situation. Where do they experience God's presence? Where are you experiencing God's presence in your life right now? If you feel so inclined, write down your reflections.

Video Reflection

Don't forget to scan the QR Code on the cover of this book for more on this topic and a mid-week spiritual practice.

Week 40 - Embracing Change: Finding Everything

....

Do not be anxious about anything, but in everything by prayer and supplication with thanksgiving let your requests be made known to God. And the peace of God, which surpasses all understanding, will guard your hearts and your minds in Christ Jesus. (Philippians 4:6-7)

Paul was no stranger to change. Think of his conversion on the road to Damascus in which he encounters the resurrected Christ (Acts 9:1-9). After this experience, he goes from being a Pharisee who is actively persecuting followers of Jesus to being the greatest evangelist in church history. While the incredible story clearly illustrates the transformation Paul experienced in his life, it appears only in the Book of Acts and not in Paul's writing. This has led most scholars to see it as an invention of the author of Acts. If Paul had truly encountered the resurrected Christ, we would expect to see at least a casual mention of it! So, we assume that the author of Acts uses this story as a narrative device to describe the enormity of Paul's change in life.

Paul's life changed dramatically when he gave up persecuting the early Church and became its most zealous advocate. He went from being the persecutor to persecuted, ultimately being imprisoned, and put to death in Rome.[2] This letter to the Church in Philippi was very likely composed while Paul was in prison.[3] Paul's encouragement to the congregation doesn't tell them that God will take away his plight or theirs. Rather, he tells of how turning to God amidst his suffering helps him to endure. He knows that ultimately worrying does no good. It solves nothing and can be debilitating. By acknowledging what we cannot change and turning it over to the universe, we can discover a peace that in many ways surpasses our understanding.

One of the most valuable elements of religion is recognizing that not everything is in our control. Even if we firmly believe in free will and self-determination, we must come to terms with the

_____

[2] While the exact details of Paul's death are not recorded in the Bible, tradition holds that he was beheaded by Emperor Nero.

[3] Phil. 1:7, 13.

reality that we cannot control everything in our lives. Instead, we must let go of some of our worries about the future and embrace the peace that comes from knowing a loving, embracing, ever-present God. Through his experience, Paul realized a sense of peace which in many ways was beyond comprehension. He lived a life that was more comfortable before he began following the teachings of Jesus, but he seemed to be sure that he made the right decision even when it cost him so much. I have a Buddhist friend who gave up a successful consulting career to live in a Tibetan monastery before coming back to the States to teach others about the value of mindfulness. He's often asked how he could give up so much in exchange for such a simple life. He often responds by saying, "I gave up nothing and found everything." Purpose in life is important. Sometimes the change to get there is difficult, but by living fully authentic lives, we can discover the peace of which scripture speaks. May it be so. Amen.

QUESTIONS

- When has turning to God, in chaotic times helped you to discover a sense of peace?

- When have you experienced a turbulent change in your life?

- What does "the peace of God" mean to you?

- How can our lives embody "the peace of God"?

- Giving up something can be difficult. When have you done so and found the decision ultimately life-enhancing?

Spiritual Practice

Each week this section on spiritual practice will entail trying something new. This week try to think about a change that you need to make in your life. Is there something that you've always wanted to try, but haven't? Is there something that you've been doing that is holding you back? If there's a change that you want or need to make, work towards it this week. If it can't be accomplished this week, or in a short time, identify and write down the steps you need to take to make it happen.

Video Reflection

Don't forget to scan the QR Code on the cover of this book for more on this topic and a mid-week spiritual practice.

RETHINKING BELIEFS

Week 41 - Rethinking Beliefs - Biblical Inerrancy

....

All scripture is inspired by God and is useful for teaching, for reproof, for correction, and for training in righteousness, so that everyone who belongs to God may be proficient, equipped for every good work. (2 Timothy 3:16-17)[1]

I'm sure that we've all heard the claim that the Bible is God's perfect, infallible, literal word. Let's be clear: the Bible is not the "inerrant word of God." In fact, making that claim is not only bad theology, but it also does a disservice to the true nature of the text. Nowhere does the Bible claim inerrancy. Of course, even if that claim were on every single page, you would have to assume that the Bible was inerrant to accept its inerrancy! The closest claim to infallibility we find in the Bible is this week's centering scripture from 2 Timothy, which many fundamentalists like to quote. As you can see from reading it, this text doesn't say that the Bible is infallible. In the text, the author[2] is giving a charge to Timothy about turning to scripture as a source of strength for the community to persevere amidst persecution. Its purpose is much more about centering on God through the stories of Jesus than it is about everything being literally true. Even if biblical inerrancy were what the author of 2 Timothy intended, he wouldn't have been writing about the Bible that we have today, because the canon wouldn't be finalized for nearly another three centuries after his lifetime! He certainly wouldn't have had access to all four Gospels that we have today or even the biblical versions of Paul's letters.[3] Furthermore, until the New Testament canon was closed, when New Testament authors wrote about "scripture," they were referring to the Hebrew Bible.

It's like what the "God" account on X (formerly Twitter) said in a popular meme, "Every word in the Bible is literally true. Then they

---

[1] *New Revised Standard Version.*

[2] Almost all scholars agree that while this epistle is credited to Paul, he didn't actually write it. It is one of three letters called "The Pastoral Epistles" which consist of 1 and 2 Timothy and Titus. See Ehrman, *The New Testament,* 385.

[3] For example, many scholars believe that 1 and 2 Corinthians are compilations of several of letters and may even contain interpolations from later authors.

start grouping themselves into sentences and you've got yourself a problem."[4] So, if the Bible isn't the inerrant word of God, what is it? The Bible is an extremely rich collection of writings from different people with different concerns writing about their experiences of God, at different times. It is not God telling us about Godself. It is written by human beings about how they understand God...and that's the case even for verses that attribute their words to God. This is why we get explanations that outright contradict each other in the Bible.[5] Do we truly want to believe in a literal way everything that is written in the Bible? For instance, Psalm 139:9 reads, "Happy shall they be who take your little ones and dash them against the rock!" Reading the entire Psalm helps us to understand that it was written from the perspective of someone during the Babylonian exile and was a cry for retribution. Surely, we wouldn't believe that such murder was literally permissible.

The Bible is much more valuable to us when we read it in its context. It helps us to gain a richer understanding of God as we read about how people have made sense of God in their lives. Some theologies that are presented are decidedly more helpful than others. We must let go of the notion that there's a unified theology of God presented throughout the Bible, because that's simply not the case. The Book of Job conveys a theology that God causes suffering that must be endured. In Ecclesiastes, we read that there's nothing better in life than to eat, drink, and be merry.[6] In some places, the Bible describes a vengeful God of wrath, and in others we find a compassionate comforter. Each of these understandings helped particular people find meaning in their own unique circumstances. The United Church of Christ's motto is that "God is still speaking." We too are still speaking—about God. May we add our voices and our understanding to the conversation. May it be so. Amen.

---

[4] God (@TheTweetofGod), X, February 9, 2019.
[5] Here's a minor example: 2 Kings 24:8 and Chronicles 36:9, texts that identify Jehoiachin as being quite differently aged when he started to rule.
[6] Ecclesiastes 8:15.

QUESTIONS

- What do you think about the idea of biblical inerrancy? How about the Bible being "inspired by" God?

- What, if anything, is lost when we embrace the humanity of the biblical text?

- What's gained by acknowledging the actual authors of the text?

- What examples of contradictions in the Bible come to your mind?

- What elements of God's character presented in the Bible are easier to let go of once we reject biblical inerrancy?

Spiritual Practice

Since the Bible is filled with words about God, not from God, why not add your voice to the mix? Sit down and write about how you understand God. What are God's characteristics? How have you experienced God in your life? You can write with bullet points or a narrative. You could also use art if that helps to express your understanding of God.

Video Reflection

Don't forget to scan the QR Code on the cover of this book for more on this topic and a mid-week spiritual practice.

Week 42 – Rethinking Beliefs: Hell

....

But I say to you that if you are angry with a brother or sister, you will be liable to judgment, and if you insult a brother or sister, you will be liable to the council, and if you say, "You fool," you will be liable to the hell of fire. (Matthew 5:22)

I'm agnostic about the idea of an afterlife, meaning that I simply do not know if there is one. I choose to live my life as if this time on Earth is the only time that I've got. One thing that I feel certain about, though, is that there is no Hell. In fact, the concept of Hell isn't biblical. It's well known that the ancient Israelites who became the Jewish people did not believe in an afterlife. New Testament scholar Bart Ehrman points out that they believed that the soul was tied to breath, which is why Genesis 2:7 defines life as beginning at first breath.[7] In the two hundred years or so before Jesus' birth, some groups within Judaism flirted with the idea of an afterlife, but by and large, people didn't believe in it. That means that most of the people to whom Jesus was speaking—and very likely Jesus himself—did not believe in an afterlife at all. Instead, Jesus' message was about the Reign of God *on Earth*, not in the sweet by-and-by somewhere in the sky.

But didn't Jesus talk about Hell...like in this week's centering scripture? Kind of. The word that Jesus used for Hell was "Gehenna," which was a literal place outside the walls of Jerusalem. This valley was long associated with child sacrifice by fire to pagan gods, hence the association with a pit of fire.[8] People in Jesus' day would have had a very strong mental image of Gehenna.

Because of this association with child sacrifice, this place was thought to be abandoned by God and was a way of speaking about a distance from God.[9] Jesus uses the notion of Gehenna as a contrast to the values of the Reign of God. The Reign of God is a place that is filled with love, compassion, welcome, kindness, peace, and justice. If you deny those values, you distance yourself from God

---

[7] Bart Ehrman, "What Jesus Really Said About Heaven and Hell," *Time*, May 8, 2020, https://time.com/5822598/jesus-really-said-heaven-hell/

[8] Ehrman, "What Jesus Really Said About Heaven and Hell."

[9] Ehrman, "What Jesus Really Said About Heaven and Hell."

and that is like being in Gehenna, a place where you can't sense God's presence. For instance, in this passage from Matthew 5, Jesus is suggesting that by holding on to anger, you are separating yourself from God, which is why Jesus spends so much time talking about forgiveness and reconciliation; those actions bring you closer to God.

If Hell isn't biblical, then where did it come from? Mostly from pagan thought and from Dante's imagination. The concept of eternal punishment simply isn't helpful. There's a meme that has circulated on social media that reads, "If you need the threat of hell to be a good person, then you're just a bad person on a leash."[10] Jesus' message isn't about doing the right thing to avoid everlasting punishment. Jesus' message isn't about believing the right thing to save your eternal soul. Jesus' message is about embracing the values of the Reign of God in such a way that it transforms your life and the world around you, here and now. People often ask me what happens to evil people in the world when they die if there is no Hell. Hitler, for example. Honestly, we don't know. But wishing them eternal punishment isn't the Christian response. While there are certain things that we as human beings may not be able to forgive, wishing someone suffering and pain is never the response that Jesus taught us. Let's be concerned about this life, and let God take care of the rest. May it be so. Amen.

QUESTIONS

- Do you believe in an afterlife?

- If so, what do you think it will be like? If not, how do you make sense of death?

- If you believe in Hell, how would letting go of the idea of eternal damnation change your theology?

- Can you think of a modern example of *Gehenna*?

- There are certainly "hells" on Earth. When have you experienced a time that felt like hell?

---

[10] Cartoonist, Paul Kinsella, *Facebook*, September 5, 2022, https://www.facebook.com/cartoonistpaukinsella/photos/a.321018391333285/4809584062476673/?type=3.

Spiritual Practice

This week, I invite you try to a meditative practice. Find a quiet place. Sit in a comfortable position with your feet flat on the ground. Take a few moments to center yourself by closing your eyes and focusing on your breath. After you feel centered, think about a difficult person in your life. Perhaps not someone who has caused you great harm, but simply someone who you have trouble dealing with. Acknowledge the difficulty. Then envision that person finding happiness. Allow yourself to experience the joy with them. Notice how you feel about yourself and that person. After a few moments, open your eyes and go about your day.

Video Reflection

Don't forget to scan the QR Code on the cover of this book for more on this topic and a mid-week spiritual practice.

Week 43 – Rethinking Beliefs: Vending Machine God

....

Jesus answered them, "Have faith in God. Truly I tell you, if you say to this mountain, 'Be taken up and thrown into the sea,' and if you do not doubt in your heart but believe that what you say will come to pass, it will be done for you. So I tell you, whatever you ask for in prayer, believe that you have received it, and it will be yours." (Mark 11:22-24)

Many Christians think of God as a cosmic vending machine into which we put our prayers, and out of which God dispenses what we've asked for. The truth is that even after we've done a lot of work deconstructing bad theology, we still believe something like this at the end of the day; we think that if we ask for it and desire it deeply enough, God will give it to us. That's simply not the way that God works. A vending machine God is about the most Americanized form of the gospel that I can fathom; we give God something (prayer) and God gives us something back (our heart's desire). This theology is transactional and reduces God to a dispenser of commodities. We need to give up the idea of God as a vending machine!

In some ways, this misinterpretation is understandable. There are multiple verses throughout the Bible encouraging us to pray; suggesting that if we do pray in just the right way, with the correct intention, our request will be granted. As with everything, context is key. For instance, this week's centering scripture is found in the context of the Monday of Holy Week and the cursing of the fig tree. In this example, Jesus has overturned the money changers' tables and spoken vigorously about the need for change in the Temple. The "mountain" that Jesus wanted to move is the purity system enforced by the Temple that divided people into social classes. The "belief" that he describes is a commitment to a more authentic religious system in which those barriers between people and God are broken down. Without this context, you can make God into a vending machine. But when you ground your understanding in the text, it's clear what Jesus means.

I'm not at all against prayer. I'm simply opposed to the way that many Christians think about it. But, if the purpose of prayer isn't a transaction, why do we pray? Early twentieth-century Scottish Baptist Minister Oswald Chambers put it like this, "To say that 'prayer changes things' is not as close to the truth as saying, 'prayer changes me and then I change things.'"[11] I believe that prayer—in whatever form it takes for us—is important. I don't think it's significant because it influences God: I think it's invaluable because it changes us. Whenever we pray, we take a moment to stop—a rarity!—and practice the values Jesus taught us. We practice caring about other people as we name the concerns that they are experiencing. We practice acknowledging small things in life that are going well when we thank God for the blessings in our lives. When we pray for those things for which we are longing, we are honest with ourselves about our motivations. When we lift up the state of our world, we have the opportunity to think about how we can make it better. Prayer teaches us mindfulness about ourselves, others, and the world in which we live. If we are expanding our self-compassion and kindness towards others, then I'm all for praying without ceasing. May it be so. Amen.

QUESTIONS

- How do you understand prayer?
- If you pray, why? If not, why not?
- If you pray, how and when do you typically do it?
- Do your prayers change the way you act or think about situations?
- How has your view and practice of prayer changed over time?

Spiritual Practice

This week, I invite you to pray in any way that is comfortable for you. As you pray, try to let go of the notion that God will do things for you. For instance, instead of saying "Please heal Sue's cancer," try saying, "May I be present with Sue and support her during this difficult time." If you pray regularly, take note of how your prayers

---

[11] Oswald Chambers, "The Purpose of Prayer," *My Utmost For His Highest,* https://utmost.org/the-purpose-of-prayer/.

change. If you don't pray regularly, try it and see if it helps you to become more mindful.

Video Reflection

Don't forget to scan the QR Code on the cover of this book for more on this topic and a mid-week spiritual practice.

Week 44 – Rethinking Beliefs:
Penal Substitutionary Atonement

....

Since all have sinned and fall short of the glory of God; they are now justified by his grace as a gift, through the redemption that is in Christ Jesus, whom God put forward as a sacrifice of atonement by his blood, effective through faith. He did this to demonstrate his righteousness, because in his divine forbearance he had passed over the sins previously committed; it was to demonstrate at the present time his own righteousness, so that he is righteous and he justifies the one who has the faith of Jesus. (Romans 3:23–26)

You might not know the phrase "penal substitutionary atonement," but I'd be willing to bet that you've encountered the theology. It goes like this: God created an imperfect humanity. God then got angry at humanity for being imperfect and needed a sacrifice to atone for humanity's sins. So, God sent God's son (who was also kind of God) to die on the cross as a sacrifice to appease God's self for humanity's imperfection. It doesn't make a whole lot of sense, does it? Even so, it has become a prominent notion within Christianity. There are certainly Bible verses that give this interpretation of Jesus' death, but it is just that—an interpretation. Jesus didn't teach this about himself and spent most of his time confronting the oppression of his people by the Roman Empire and the corruption of the religious establishment, which is what ultimately got him killed.

If you read through the historic creeds of the church, you'll notice that they're focused on what Christians should believe about Jesus' birth, death, and resurrection. They completely leave out one very important detail: Jesus' life! We Christians ought to be more focused on what we know about Jesus' life on Earth than on the theology that surrounds his death. Jesus didn't live to die for humanity's sins. Jesus lived in such a way that he was executed by the ruling state. He didn't die *for* humanity's sins: he died *because of* humanity's sins. Jesus spent his life speaking the truth in love to the principalities and the powers. You don't get to confront the most powerful empire on Earth and come out unscathed. He spoke, albeit sometimes covertly, about Roman occupation and oppression of his people. He also spent much of his time actively disobeying the purity laws enforced by the religious establishment that divided his people into classes. Jesus took on the rich and the powerful; and that had real, concrete consequences.

Is anything lost if we give up the notion of penal substitutionary atonement? The Temple in Jerusalem practiced atonement through animal sacrifices to God. The thought was that God would be so angry with our wrongdoing that God would need some kind of gift to forgive the wrongdoer. This was a common belief in the ancient world. Later Christians adapted this theology and applied it to Jesus as a one-time sacrifice. Jesus took issue with many Temple practices, including atonement theology. On the Monday of Holy Week, Jesus went into the Temple and overturned the moneychangers' tables. These tables were in the Temple so that people could purchase animals and incense to sacrifice to God to perform the required religious rituals. Jesus had clearly read the prophets' words about burnt offerings and fasting![12] It's a bit odd that we have an example of Jesus outright confronting atonement theology and then having his followers apply it to him. Giving up this theology saves us from thinking that Jesus' death "saves" us from all our wrongdoings. Instead, his ministry teaches us how to live. May that be what inspires us to be better people. May it be so. Amen.

QUESTIONS

- What do you believe was the purpose of Jesus' death?

- How have your views of Jesus' crucifixion changed over time?

- Do Christians need to believe that Jesus died for our sins? Why or why not?

- What do you make of the idea of resurrection?

- Why do you think there's often more focus on Jesus' death than his life?

---

[12] Amos 5:21–24, Isaiah 58:6–7, for example.

Spiritual Practice

Art can be a powerful way to connect with God. Find a representation of a point in Jesus' life before his crucifixion. Spend some time with the image. How does it speak to you? What about the image might have been threatening to those in positions of power? If the artistic work is meaningful to you, consider purchasing a print or replica that you might place somewhere so you can see it often.

Video Reflection

Don't forget to scan the QR Code on the cover of this book for more on this topic and a mid-week spiritual practice.

GRATITUDE

Week 45 – Gratitude: God is Love, All the Time

....

Acclaim YHWH[1] with joy, all the earth! Serve YHWH with
gladness! Enter into God's presence with a joyful song! Know
that YHWH is God! YHWH made us, and we belong to the
Creator; we are God's people and the sheep of God's pasture.
Enter God's gates with thanksgiving and the courts with praise!
Give thanks to God! Bless God's Name! For YHWH is good;
God's steadfast love endures forever, and God's faithfulness to
all generations. (Psalm 100)[2]

One common call and response between the clergy and the
congregation in many congregations goes like this: the worship
leader says, "God is good" and the people respond, "All the time."
Then the leader says, "All the time" and the people respond, "God
is good." Yet given all the evil and violence in the world, it can be
hard to believe that God is always good. Most of us don't have a
well-defined theodicy (understanding of why evil exists in the
world). Here's the theological trap: If God is the supreme source
of good, yet is all-knowing and all-powerful, why is there evil in
the world? Is there a cosmic source of evil—a Devil—that God
is fighting? Is God the cause of suffering, as some sort of cosmic
plan in which everything happens for a reason? Is God the Creator
who set things into motion and then stepped back and disengaged
from human existence? Is evil a product of the Original Sin in the
Garden of Eden?

All the theological doctrines that I just listed (the Devil, God
causing suffering, a detached God, and Original Sin) are held by
many Christians, yet are abhorrent theology. Over and over in the
Bible we see God defined as "love." If God is love, then those places
in the world where we see love, are God manifested. We often want
to anthropomorphize God into a perceivable being, but that's not
the most helpful way to understand the Divine Mystery. Suppose
we see God as an energy that exists in our world and we recognize
that becoming more attuned to that energy helps us to act in more

---

[1] YHWH stands for "Yahweh" the proper name for God in the Hebrew Bible. It is often translated as "LORD."

[2] Priests for Equality, *The Inclusive Bible: The First Egalitarian Transla-*
tion.

caring, compassionate, forgiving, and ultimately loving ways, then the question of why there is evil in the world is simple to answer. Those who are not attuned to the force of love in the universe are often primarily concerned with self-interest rather than living for the benefit of the world.

The nice thing about defining God as an energy of love in the world is that it is a definition that is true whether you believe in it or not. It transcends religious tradition or dogma. You don't need to be a Christian, Muslim, Hindu, Buddhist, or a Jew to recognize that love ought to be the guiding force of our lives together. Love helps us to release self-centeredness, greed, bitterness, and resentment. Love causes us to expand acceptance and welcome. Love is an undeniable energy that exists in our world and is how both Jesus and the Bible define God. When I enter a church or nature or anywhere else where one might worship the living God, I do it with thanksgiving and praise. When I do so I am not declaring loyalty to an omniscient, omnipotent deity. No; I am declaring allegiance to the force of love in the world. I am committing to live my life according to that love made manifest through the teachings of Jesus. God is always good, because loving is always the right thing to do. But maybe the refrain would be more powerful if it went like this: "God is Love, all the time" and "All the time, God is love." May it be so. Amen.

QUESTIONS

- How do you make sense of evil in the world?
- How do you personally define God?
- Is the definition of God as a force of love in the world adequate? Why or why not?
- When you worship God, what does that mean for you?
- What does it mean to give thanks to God?

Spiritual Practice

This month we are focusing on gratitude. Try keeping a gratitude jar this month. Find a jar and every time something happens for which you are grateful, write it down on a small piece of paper and put it in the jar. Try to do this at least once a day. You might also say a prayer as you drop it in. Perhaps, "Great source of love, thank you."

Video Reflection

Don't forget to scan the QR Code on the cover of this book for more on this topic and a mid-week spiritual practice.

Week 46 – Gratitude: Lessons from Paul

*I have learned to be content with whatever I have. I know
what it is to have little, and I know what it is to have plenty.
In any and all circumstances I have learned the secret of being
well-fed and of going hungry, of having plenty and of being
in need. I can do all things through him who strengthens me.
(Philippians 4:11b–13)*

Paul is an interesting, frequently venerated, oft-misunderstood
figure. He lived his life confidently, yet his views were dynamic.
He vehemently advocated ideas that were ultimately wrong (i.e.,
that the world would end in his lifetime), yet the trajectory of his
life was drastically altered by his experience with the teachings
of Jesus. Paul came from a place of relative privilege as both a
pharisee and a Roman citizen,[3] but he put it all on the line to lead a
nomadic life starting churches throughout the ancient Near East.
He was arrested and sentenced to death because of his faith. His
rhetoric could come off as extremely harsh and, in some places,
even hateful, ultimately, he was more passionate than hateful
and his letters came from a place of deep care and concern for the
communities he founded.

The last section of Philippians demonstrates the side of Paul that
many of us wish we saw more often. In Philippians 4, he thanks
Euodia and Syntyche for their ministry beside him. These are two
women Paul names as "co-workers" (v.3). I'm convinced that the
misogyny often attributed to Paul is the result of interpolated
verses,[4] because he truly seems to have believed that everyone was
equal in the body of Christ, and he frequently praises women in
leadership. He then tells the community how much he appreciates
their ongoing support, especially when he is struggling. He is
almost certainly writing this letter in prison, and he's coming to
terms with the price that he paid for his faith.

---

[3] Acts 16:37–38, 22:25–28 claim that Paul was a Roman citizen,
but he doesn't make this claim himself in his epistles, so there is some
debate among scholars about the historical accuracy of his citizenship.
Regardless, as a Pharisee, Paul would have been in a position of authority and had a more comfortable life.

[4] Interpolations are verses that are added by later editors.

In Paul's own words, he admits to having known times of plenty and times when he had very little. For Paul, it is his unwavering faith that helps him to get through. With Paul's zeal, it's unsurprising that his commitment to faith is a source of inspiration and encouragement. I don't know about you, but I often don't feel as confident in my faith as Paul does in his. I frequently have times of doubt, especially in difficult times. Even though we may long to believe in a God who will solve our worries in times of difficulty, I think it's ultimately not helpful simply to hope that God will make everything better. Instead, we can learn a great deal from Paul by noting to whom he turns for support in difficult times—his community. He writes to the Philippians, in part, to thank them for continuing to be there for him through the difficulties. Our communities are different depending on our circumstances. We might find our communities through family, chosen family, friends, church, neighborhoods, or social groups; however, it is our fellow human beings who can help to support us even when our worlds feel as if they are collapsing around us. That is how God is present in our suffering. God is in the face of our neighbor and that realization can help us to get through almost anything. May it be so. Amen.

QUESTIONS

- When life is difficult, how do you cope?

- To whom do you turn for support?

- When have you experienced God's presence through community?

- Do you believe that God can ease your suffering? Why or why not?

- When have there been times in your life when your gratitude has carried you through, even though you were experiencing challenges?

Spiritual Practice

In this section, we are focusing on gratitude. How's the gratitude jar coming along? If you neglected to place notes in the gratitude jar last week, try to make an intentional effort to do so over the next few days. This week, focus on the way you experience God through others. Think about the interactions with people in which you experience God and take notice of them. Let those experiences influence what you put in your gratitude jar.

Video Reflection

Don't forget to scan the QR Code on the cover of this book for more on this topic and a mid-week spiritual practice.

Week 47 – Gratitude: Grateful as a Leper

....

As [Jesus] entered a village, ten lepers approached him.
Keeping their distance, they called out, saying, 'Jesus, Master,
have mercy on us!' When he saw them, he said to them, 'Go
and show yourselves to the priests.' And as they went, they
were made clean. Then one of them, when he saw that he
was healed, turned back, praising God with a loud voice. He
prostrated himself at Jesus' feet and thanked him. And he was
a Samaritan. Then Jesus asked, 'Were not ten made clean? But
the other nine, where are they? Was none of them found to
return and give praise to God except this foreigner?' Then he
said to him, 'Get up and go on your way; your faith has made
you well.' (Luke 17:12–19)[5]

I've preached on this story from Luke many times, but the most
impactful time was when I gave a first-person character sermon
from the perspective of the grateful leper. I like to do these sermons
occasionally, because acting out the story helps me to understand
the characters better. This person, plagued with leprosy, only gets
eight or so verses in the New Testament, yet his story is striking.
What would it have been like to live with a disease in a period in
which there was limited medicine? How would it have felt to be
ostracized by society? How might I react if I could suddenly return
to the people who had cast me aside?

"Leprosy" wasn't necessarily "Hansen's disease," which is how we
would define leprosy today. Instead, it could have been any number
of skin ailments. People with these conditions were forced out of
villages to stop contamination, which—while tragic—was also an
understandable response for the sake of public health. In this time
of limited scientific understanding, it was also assumed that people
were sick because of the wrongs that they had done. There was a
rigid purity system in Jesus' world, and to participate in much of
society—especially religious rights—you had to be ritually pure.
If you became defiled, it meant that you had to go through a whole
host of rituals to regain your purity before God and society. The
priests were, of course, in charge of granting the purity.

---

[5] *New Revised Standard Version.*

A primary focus of Jesus' ministry was confronting this purity system, which divided people into classes. He recognized that the purity system was deeply flawed because even if people were physically ill, it didn't affect their purity before God. Read through the gospels and you'll notice that much of Jesus' healing has to do with forgiving sins. The traditional understanding of Jesus takes this at face value: the person had done something wrong that made them sick, Jesus forgave them their sins, and then they were made well. I think an understanding more consonant with the original purpose of the text and the historical Jesus would be that he knew people were not sick because of their sins and so he offered them forgiveness within their own understanding of the purity system. As a rabbi, that forgiveness made them ritually pure, they were "healed" according to the religious law, even if they were still afflicted with the condition. Jesus did this to contest the purity system and healed them spiritually, even if they remained physically ill. In this week's centering scripture, it is the foreigner—the most marginalized, the person with the least—who comes back to thank Jesus because he recognizes how much Jesus has given him. The gospel message isn't that Jesus will heal all our woes: it is that God doesn't abandon us when we are suffering. God claims us, and holds us tight, and that is enough. May it be so. Amen.

QUESTIONS

- How do you deal with the notion of sin in the Bible?

- How do you understand sin in your own life?

- How would it reshape your notion of sin if you saw forgiveness of sin as contesting the need to be perfectly pure?

- When have you forgiven someone even though you didn't want to?

- When has someone forgiven you even though you didn't feel you deserved it?

Spiritual Practice

This month we are focusing on gratitude. Continue placing notes in the gratitude jar. This week, try to find examples of forgiveness. Have you forgiven someone this week? Has someone forgiven you? The examples don't have to be big; they can be minor. Pay attention, write them down and place them in the gratitude jar.

Video Reflection

Don't forget to scan the QR Code on the cover of this book for more on this topic and a mid-week spiritual practice.

Week 48 – Gratitude: Mixed Emotions

....

And all the people responded with a great shout when they praised the Lord, because the foundation of the house of the Lord was laid. But many of the priests and Levites and heads of families, old people who had seen the first house on its foundations, wept with a loud voice when they saw this house, though many shouted aloud for joy, so that the people could not distinguish the sound of the joyful shout from the sound of the people's weeping, for the people shouted so loudly that the sound was heard far away. (Ezra 3:11b–13)[6]

I love the third chapter of the Book of Ezra. While not many might point to this chapter as one of their favorites, it's incredibly poignant. This week's centering scripture is part of a story in Ezra that takes place right after the Exile. In 597 BCE,[7] the Babylonians conquered the Kingdom of Judah and deported the king and nobles from Judah to Babylon. In 586 BCE, the Babylonians besieged Jerusalem and destroyed the Temple. Over the next several years, they took many prominent citizens from their homes to Babylon; the Babylonians forced them to leave everything they knew, beginning the period known as the Exile. It wasn't until 539 BCE that Cyrus the Great of Persia conquered Babylon, and in 538 BCE the people of Judah were allowed to return to their homeland.[8] As soon as they were home, work began on a new Temple, which they sought to make even more beautiful than the first.

The Book of Ezra tells the story of the new Temple's construction. In Ezra 3, the foundation of the new temple had been built and it was time for the dedication. It was going to be an incredible celebration! The priests stood on the foundation in their finest vestments, the trumpeters blasted their joyful song, cymbals clashed, and people sang boisterously. Amid all the raucous celebration, something odd happened: some people began to wail. It creates some cognitive dissonance at first to imagine these two

---

[6] *New Revised Standard Version.*

[7] The acronym BCE stands for "Before the Common Era" and CE stands for "Common Era." Scholars now typically use these abbreviations instead of BC and AD.

[8] Collins, *Introduction to the Hebrew Bible,* 14.

groups of people occupying the same space. Those wailing were the ones who remembered the other Temple and the days before the Exile. They weren't simply remembering what had been; they were also mourning those who were now gone since they had last stood at the Temple. The realization of all that they had lost was what prompted their wailing. Ezra says that it became so loud that people could no longer distinguish between the wailing and the shouting, between the sadness and the joy—their voices mingled as one in a loud roar.

This story certainly speaks to the fact that different people within a community are often not in the same place emotionally, but I think it also speaks to our own ability to experience mixed emotions. There can be times in our lives—even when things are going well and we are grateful—when we experience a bittersweet sentiment, and our emotions blend together. It is very much like those gathered at the Temple steps; grateful to be home and surrounded by loved ones, yet also longing deeply for what used to be.

Allowing our wailing and shouting to blend can be powerful. There's also significance in recognizing that the moment we're in is a gift that won't ever come again. Sometimes when our wailing overcomes our shouting, it can help us to take a breath, look around, and recenter ourselves in gratitude. May it be so. Amen.

QUESTIONS

- At what times of the year do you typically feel mixed emotions?

- In which seasons do you feel particularly joyful?

- How do you cope when the wailing in your life overcomes the shouting?

- When you have experienced times when it seemed as if everything was falling apart?

- How do you re-center gratitude when life is difficult?

Spiritual Practice

This month we are focusing on gratitude. Continue placing notes in the gratitude jar. This week pay particular attention to your emotions. What caused you to feel joy this week? At the end of the week, open your gratitude jar and read all the notes that you've written over the course of the past few weeks. Notice how you feel as you read them.

Video Reflection

Don't forget to scan the QR Code on the cover of this book for more on this topic and a mid-week spiritual practice.

CHRISTMAS

Week 49 – Christmas: Luke's Version
··

*In those days a decree went out from Caesar Augustus that all
the world should be registered. This was the first registration
and was taken while Quirinius was governor of Syria. All
went to their own towns to be registered. Joseph also went from
the town of Nazareth in Galilee to Judea, to the city of David
called Bethlehem, because he was descended from the house
and family of David. He went to be registered with Mary, to
whom he was engaged and who was expecting a child. While
they were there, the time came for her to deliver her child. And
she gave birth to her firstborn son and wrapped him in bands
of cloth and laid him in a manger, because there was no place
in the guest room. (Luke 2:1-7)*

There's much to unpack about how we speak of Jesus' birth at
Christmas. Two of the gospels do not contain birth narratives.
Mark begins with Jesus' baptism and John begins with a poetic
theological argument about Jesus' preexistence with God. The
story that we often tell is a conglomeration of Luke and Matthew's
respective narratives. The stories are different and serve different
purposes. Neither story is historically accurate, but both strive to
express theological truth. Luke's version is a tool for foreshadowing
Jesus' emphasis on justice for the marginalized.

In this version, the emperor sends out a decree for people to
return to their homelands to be registered for tax purposes. This
is ahistorical because you would want to tax people where they
currently live, not where they were born. The census primarily
serves as a literary device to get Jesus from Nazareth to Bethlehem
where the Messiah was supposed to be born.[1] It narratively displays
the power of the Roman Empire to affect the lives of its subjects.
Jesus was born in simple circumstances, surrounded by animals,
and placed in the animals' feeding trough as a crib. Shepherds
then visit Jesus—people who were a low social class and who lived
outside with their animals. By narrating Jesus' birth in simple

[1] Jesus was likely born in Nazareth, and both Matthew and Luke's
accounts of Jesus' birth in Bethlehem are, I think, attempts to affirm
that Jesus is meeting the messianic requirement of a birth in Bethlehem.

circumstances and depicting a low social class of visitors coming to honor him, Luke shows us that the focus of Jesus' ministry will be standing up for those who have very little. This means that while Luke's narrative isn't a *factual* story, it is a *true* story.

Luke's narrative of events also gives Mary a great deal of autonomy.[2] In this version, the angel visits Mary and she gives consent to carry the holy child. In Mary's prayer of gratitude that has become known as the "Magnificat," her words likewise pay attention to the marginalized. She says, "He has shown strength with his arm; he has scattered the proud in the thoughts of their hearts. He has brought down the powerful from their thrones, and lifted up the lowly; he has filled the hungry with good things, and sent the rich away empty."[3] As we journey toward Christmas, let's remember that this story is about Jesus' concern for those in need from the very beginning of his life. Let's hold that concern for those in need close to our own hearts too and remember that there is no Christmas without it. May it be so. Amen

QUESTIONS

- How does viewing Matthew and Luke's narratives about Jesus' birth as separate stories affect your view of Christmas?

- If Jesus wasn't born in Bethlehem, would it change how you view him?

- What does it mean that Mary has autonomy in Luke's Gospel?

- What do you think about the notion of the virgin birth?

- What message do you take from the Magnificat?

Spiritual Practice

Many Christian communities use candlelight to journey symbolically toward Christmas. You'll need five candles and a

---

[2] Also note that Mary would not have been a virgin. The Hebrew word in Isaiah to which the Gospel writers refer didn't mean virgin, it meant "young woman."

[3] Luke 1:51–53.

wreath for this week's practice. Place the wreath and candles somewhere where you can see them throughout the week. Consider getting three light blue candles (a color symbolizing hope), a pink candle (to symbolize joy), and a white candle (for Jesus) to place in the center. Today light one of the blue candles for hope. What makes you feel hopeful? Perhaps you could make a list of what feels hopeful about your life, your family, your community, and your world. Take a moment to enjoy the light of the candle.

Video Reflection

Don't forget to scan the QR Code on the cover of this book for more on this topic and a mid-week spiritual practice.

Week 50 – Christmas: Matthew's Version

Now after they had left, an angel of the Lord appeared to Joseph in a dream and said, "Get up, take the child and his mother, and flee to Egypt, and remain there until I tell you, for Herod is about to search for the child, to destroy him." Then Joseph got up, took the child and his mother by night, and went to Egypt and remained there until the death of Herod. This was to fulfill what had been spoken by the Lord through the prophet, "Out of Egypt I have called my son." (Matthew 2:13-15)

Matthew's version of events often takes a back seat to Luke's narrative in the combined Christmas story that we typically tell. In Matthew's Gospel, Jesus' family is already in Bethlehem, and he is born in a house. We lose the narrative about the census, the guest room, shepherds, and angels. Instead, it is magi (astrologers, wise men) from the East who are tasked with predicting the future. This is significant for Matthew, because his main priority throughout his gospel is to show that Jesus is the fulfillment of Jewish scripture. When the magi bring gifts fit for a king, Matthew signifies that Jesus is the Messiah, who was supposed to be a warrior/king.

Matthew's Gospel is more Jewish than Mark, Luke, or John, reflecting the community for which he is writing. One of the most evident motives is Matthew's desire to show that Jesus is the new Moses. We can see this very clearly in the way that Matthew structures the birth narrative. Herod orders the slaughter of Israelite children (just as the Pharoah had in Exodus). The Holy Family travels from Judea to Egypt just as the ancient Israelites had done, the place where Moses' story began. Once Herod had died, the family traveled back up to Judea, just as Moses led the ancient Israelites out of Egypt to the promised land. You can see other parallels throughout the gospel. Recall how Jesus goes to a mountain—just as Moses did to receive the Ten Commandments— to give a new law in the Sermon on the Mount. Matthew has a clear agenda to show Jesus as the fulfillment of Hebrew Bible prophecy and a new interpreter of God's law; the theological implications are profound.

In Matthew's Christmas narrative, Jesus and his family flee persecution from an oppressive government and become refugees in Egypt. Egypt accepts the family without question and allows its members to live as refugees in their land. It is only once the family no longer fears political persecution that they can return to their homeland. Since there is no evidence of a massacre of children by Herod, it's unlikely that any of this ever happened. However, it is significant that the author chose to portray Jesus' birth narrative this way. It signifies truth beyond fact. The story of families fleeing violence in their homeland in search of safety and a better life is a story that many refugees in today's world know all too well. Later in this gospel, Jesus instructs us that when we care for the "least of these," we are in fact caring for him.[4] This narrative appropriately reminds us that whenever refugees have these horrific experiences, it is as if Christ is suffering with them as well. To be blunt, God calls us to care for refugees as if they are the Holy Family coming into our land, because in a very real way, they are. May it be so. Amen.

QUESTIONS

- What do you learn from Matthew's narrative of Jesus' birth?
- What other parallels do you see in Matthew's Gospel between Jesus and Moses?
- What different message does Matthew send by having magi rather than shepherds visit Jesus?
- If Jesus is on the side of the oppressed and vulnerable, where do you see Jesus in our world today?
- How does it change our perspective on Matthew's Gospel if we keep it separate from Luke's?

Spiritual Practice

This week, continue the spiritual practice of lighting a candle on the advent wreath. Today, light a blue candle for peace in addition to the candle from last week that is already burning. Where are

[4] Matthew 25.

the places in our world most in need of peace? How about in your life? In what ways can you be a peacemaker? Take a moment to enjoy the light of the candles.

Video Reflection

Don't forget to scan the QR Code on the cover of this book for more on this topic and a mid-week spiritual practice.

Week 51 – Christmas: Women in the Genealogy

....

*Abraham was the father of Isaac, and Isaac the father of Jacob,
and Jacob the father of Judah and his brothers, and Judah the
father of Perez and Zerah by Tamar...and Salmon the father
of Boaz by Rahab, and Boaz the father of Obed by Ruth, and
Obed the father of Jesse, and Jesse the father of King David.
And David was the father of Solomon by the wife of Uriah...
and Jacob the father of Joseph the husband of Mary, who bore
Jesus, who is called the Messiah. (Matthew 1:1-16, selections)*

Let's be honest, if we're reading through the Bible, we often skip
the genealogies in Matthew and Luke, don't we? I know that I do!
It's hard to sit and read through a list of seemingly irrelevant
names. Matthew and Luke's genealogies are different from each
other both in content and purpose. Luke begins with Jesus and
traces his lineage all the way back through David (from whom the
Messiah had to be descended) to Adam and then ultimately to God.
Luke wants to show that Jesus is of God and was born for the good
of all people. Matthew is writing to a primarily Jewish audience
and wants to show that Jesus is the fulfillment of the Hebrew
scripture. As such, he begins with Abraham who was the father of
Judaism. There's a lot that can be said about Matthew's genealogy,
but there's one particularly noteworthy thing: Matthew includes
five women in the genealogy! Genealogies were typically only done
from father to son, and this move has confounded theologians for
almost two thousand years.

These women weren't chosen at random, either. Each of these
women was entangled in some kind of sexual scandal. Tamar's
husband died, and after his brothers failed to provide her with
an heir, she had to dress up as a prostitute and trick her father-
in-law Judah into sleeping with her to get her pregnant.[5] Rahab
was a prostitute who hid the Israelite spies entering Jericho.[6] Ruth

---

[5] Genesis 38. In that society, there was a "levirate obligation" in
which a male relative needed to get the widow pregnant to ensure a
biological heir if there had not been male child with the now deceased
husband.
[6] Joshua 2.

seduced her wealthy relative Boaz to survive.[7] The "wife of Uriah" is Bathsheba whom King David raped.[8]/[9] Mary was an unwed teen mother whom Joseph was planning to leave before an angel stopped him, in Matthew's birth narrative.[10]/[11] It's also worth noting that all the women except Mary are Gentiles.

Why are these women included? These women became the center of their stories and found a way to survive amid difficult circumstances. These are the women from whom Jesus comes. Even though there was a sexual scandal surrounding Mary, those were the people through whom God was working. This also foreshadowed that Jesus would grow up to break down social barriers with both women and gentiles in his ministry. The women in Jesus' genealogy deserve to be acknowledged! In these years after the #metoo Movement, we have only begun to realize the sexual exploitation of women that has been swept under the rug. A lesson we can learn from the women in Jesus' genealogy is to break the silence on any injustice occurring towards women in our world. May it be so. Amen.

QUESTIONS

- Does it shift your view of Jesus' birth to know about the women in his genealogy?

- Can you think of other women in the Bible who became the center of the narrative, despite male editors cutting many women out of the stories?

- In what ways do we continue to exploit women in our society?

- How can we create systemic change to make the world more just for women?

---

[7] Ruth 3.

[8] 2 Samuel 11–12.

[9] David also ensured that her husband Uriah was killed in battle. She is likely listed as the "wife of Uriah" rather than by name to remind us of the injustice that occurred towards her.

[10] Matthew 1:18–25.

[11] The concept of "virginity" was a literary device used to foreshadow that someone was going to live a great life and was likely built on a mistranslation of a Hebrew word that means "young woman," not "virgin."

- Jesus broke down barriers between genders in his society. What gender barriers do we still need to dismantle?

Spiritual Practice

This week, continue with the spiritual practice of lighting a candle on the advent wreath. Today, light the pink candle for joy in addition to the candles from previous weeks that are already burning. Where in your life are you experiencing joy? Where in the world do you see joy? Take a moment to enjoy the light of the candles.

Video Reflection

Don't forget to scan the QR Code on the cover of this book for more on this topic and a mid-week spiritual practice.

Week 52 – Christmas: Dragons for Christmas

....

A great portent appeared in heaven: a woman clothed with the sun, with the moon under her feet, and on her head a crown of twelve stars. She was pregnant and was crying out in birth pangs, in the agony of giving birth. Then another portent appeared in heaven: a great red dragon, with seven heads and ten horns, and seven diadems on his heads. His tail swept down a third of the stars of heaven and threw them to the earth. Then the dragon stood before the woman who was about to bear a child, so that he might devour her child as soon as it was born. And she gave birth to a son, a male child, who is to rule all the nations with a scepter of iron. But her child was snatched away and taken to God and to his throne. (Revelation 12:1-5)

Everyone knows about the birth narratives in Matthew and Luke, but did you know that there was a birth narrative in the Book of Revelation? Since the story is found in the oft-misunderstood Book of Revelation, is there any surprise that it's weird? Many Christians think that Revelation is about predicting an apocalyptic end of the world, but it isn't. Revelation was written by an author named John on the island of Patmos, and he tried to make sense of the world in which he lived. He used fantastical writing to speak the truth about an empire that was actively persecuting his fellow Jesus followers, which is exactly what's happening in this story. John reappropriates a Greco-Roman myth to speak about the evils of an empire.

In Greco-Roman mythology, Zeus comes down and sleeps with a human named Leto. She becomes pregnant with their son Apollo (the god of light). As she is about to give birth, a giant monster named Python lies in wait to devour the child—until Zeus swoops in and saves them. In John's retelling, Mary prepares to give birth to Jesus, but a seven-headed red dragon prepares to devour the child, which is a representation of Rome (the city of *seven* hills whose soldiers wore red clothing). What's more, elsewhere in Revelation the dragon is said to have lost a battle in heaven and is sent to Earth to rule as a city with seven hills. The Roman emperor was said to be the "Son of God"; he was the son of the god Apollo.

By taking the birth narrative of Caesar's family and making it about Jesus, John performs a clever reversal. It is no longer Apollo, and thus Caesar, who are being *saved* by the monster. Rather they have *become* the monster that is seeking to swallow up Jesus and his followers. What's more, Apollo, Caesar, and the Roman Empire are not the light of the world: Christ is the true light of the world.[12]

I think this has become my favorite birth narrative in the Bible. In it, we see Jesus at odds with an empire from the very beginning. Ultimately, Jesus' life was focused on proclaiming a world counter to the one that Rome had created. In Jesus' vision for the future, peace is achieved through the presence of justice and not through conquest and violence. Jesus' ministry focused on how peace through justice could be attained through loyalty to the Reign of God instead of any nation-state or empire. For that message, Jesus was crucified. The purpose of the birth narrative in Revelation and the message of Christmas is we should proclaim the hope, peace, joy, and love that we have learned from the life and teachings of Jesus, and seek to embody those values in our lives. If we can do that year-round, we will certainly create a different kind of world. May it be so. Amen.

QUESTIONS

- If you read the Book of Revelation as an anti-imperial text rather than an apocalyptic one, does it change the meaning for you?

- Are there other places in the biblical text where you notice the presence of Greco-Roman myths?

- Which of the birth narratives resonates most with you? Why?

- How can we confront the imperialism we see in twenty-first-century America?

- What should we learn from the birth narratives? How should those affect our faith throughout the year?

---

[12] Borg and Crossan, *The First Christmas*, 193–96.

Spiritual Practice

This week, continue the spiritual practice of lighting a candle on the advent wreath. Today light the last blue candle symbolizing love; in addition to the candles from previous weeks that are already burning. Where are the places in your life where love is needed? Are there places of hurt that love, compassion, forgiveness, and reconciliation could heal? Where do you feel love most strongly at this moment? Take a moment to enjoy the light of the candles. On Christmas Eve or Christmas Day, light the white candle in the center of the wreath.

Video Reflection

Don't forget to scan the QR Code on the cover of this book for more on this topic and a mid-week spiritual practice.

CONCLUSION

We've journeyed together for fifty-two weeks, and I hope it has been a meaningful trek for you! I expect that you have learned more about scripture, Jesus' ministry, and your own spirituality along the way. Some spiritual practices have likely been a stretch, while others may have resonated deeply. If you have found something you like, continue to explore it! Don't be afraid to try new spiritual practices, either. In experimenting, we can find what sustains us. Consider using the book again and allowing yourself to enter the practices more deeply. If the devotional was meaningful for you, consider facilitating a small group and using the book as a guide. I hope this is simply the beginning of a deeper spiritual journey for you.

Part of becoming awakened is realizing that there is always more to learn. The world needs more caring, compassionate, and understanding people. The Progressive Christian Movement is truly about reclaiming the authentic teachings of Jesus and letting go of the theological baggage of inherited bad theology. In doing so, we strive to progress closer to Jesus' vision of the Reign of God. One of the most important realizations we can have as people of faith is that working for a peaceful, just, and inclusive society is a way in which we can live fully into the values that Jesus taught. I hope you have experienced an inward awakening that will lead to outward action. Do you feel like the one sheep on the book's cover, yet? Are you able to see the needs of the world in ways that others can't? Are you awakened? May we all continue to strive towards greater awakening. May it be so. Amen.

BIBLIOGRAPHY

Ackerman, Susan. *When Heroes Love: The Ambiguity of Eros In The Stories Of Gilgamesh And David*. New York: Columbia University Press, 2005.

Act As If... Sermon. All Saints Church, Pasadena, 2016. https://www.youtube.com/watch?v=0ttMLXcTuiA&t=50s.

"Atom." In *Wikipedia*, n.d. https://en.wikipedia.org/wiki/Atom#:~:text=Atoms%20are%20extremely%20small%2C%20typically,see%20atoms%20with%20conventional%20microscopes.

Baldwin, James. "The Doom and Glory of Knowing Who You Are." *Life Magazine*, May 24, 1963.

Borg, Marcus. "Christians in an Age of Empire, Then and Now." The Marcus Borg Foundation, May 17, 2008. https://marcusjborg.org/videos/christians-in-an-age-of-empire-then-and-now/.

———. *Meeting Jesus Again for the First Time: The Historical Jesus & The Heart Of Contemporary Faith*. San Francisco: HarperSanFrancisco, 1994.

Borg, Marcus, and John Dominic Crossan. *The First Christmas: What the Gospels Really Teach About Jesus's Birth*. New York: HarperOne, 2007.

———. *The Last Week: What the Gospels Really Teach About Jesus's Final Days in Jerusalem*. New York: HarperOne, 2006.

Cartoonist, Paul Kinsella. *Facebook* (blog), September 5, 2022. https://www.facebook.com/cartoonistpaukinsella/photos/a.321018391333285/4809584062476673/?type=3.

Chambers, Oswald. "The Purpose of Prayer." My Utmost For His Highest, n.d. https://utmost.org/the-purpose-of-prayer/.

Collins, John J. *Introduction to the Hebrew Bible*. Minneapolis: Fortress Press, 2004.

Constitution of the United States of America (n.d.). https://constitution.congress.gov/constitution/amendment-1/.

Ehrman, Bart. *The New Testament: A Historical Introduction to the Early Christian Writings*. 3rd ed. Oxford: Oxford University Press, 2004.

———. "What Jesus Really Said About Heaven and Hell." *Time* (blog), May 8, 2020. https://time.com/5822598/jesus-really-said-heaven-hell/.

Enns, Pete. "The Bible for Normal People," n.d. https://thebiblefornormalpeople.com/episode-228-emilie-townes-the-wisdom-of-hope-reissue/.

Esposito, John L. *Islam: The Straight Path*. Oxford: Oxford University Press, 2011.

Fox, Matthew. *Original Blessing: A Primer in Creation Spirituality*. Santa Fe: Bear & Company, 1983.

Funk, Robert W., Roy W. Hoover, and The Jesus Seminar. *The Five Gospels: The Search for the Authentic Words of Jesus*. San Francisco: HarperSanFrancisco, 1993.

God (@TheTweetofGod). *X* (blog), February 9, 2019. twitter.com/tweetofGod.

Horner, Tom M. *Jonathan Loved David: Homosexuality in Biblical Times*. Louisville: The Westminster John Knox Press, 1978.

Israel Finkelstein, and Neil Asher Silberman. *The Bible Unearthed: Archaeology's New Vision of Ancient Israel and the Origin of Its Sacred Texts*. New York: Free Press, 2001.

Kearns, Shanoon. "I Am A Deviant." *Queer Theology* (blog), n.d. https://www.queertheology.com/i-am-a-deviant/.

Kraybill, J. Nelson. "To Hell with the Pigs!" *Anabaptist World* (blog), August 17, 2015. https://anabaptistworld.org/to-hell-with-the-pigs/#:~:text=That%20was%20the%20term%20for,occupying%20force%20was%20%E2%80%94%20a%20pig.

Levine, Amy-Jill. "Amy-Jill Levine: How to Read the Bible's 'Clobber Passages' on Homosexuality." *Outreach* (blog), September 12, 2022. https://outreach.faith/2022/09/amy-jill-levine-how-to-read-the-bibles-clobber-passages-on-homosexuality/.

Molloy, Michael. *Experiencing The World's Religion's: Tradition, Challenge, and Change.* 3rd ed. New York: McGraw-Hill, 2005.

NASA Hubble Mission Team. "New Horizons Spacecraft Answers Question: How Dark Is Space?," January 13, 2021. https://science.nasa.gov/missions/hubble/new-horizons-spacecraft-answers-question-how-dark-is-space/.

National Institute on Mental Health. "Mental Illness," 2023. https://www.nimh.nih.gov/health/statistics/mental-illness#:~:text=Mental%20illnesses%20are%20common%20in,(57.8%20million%20in%202021).

Pew Research Center. "On the Intersection of Science and Religion," August 26, 2020. https://www.pewresearch.org/religion/2020/08/26/on-the-intersection-of-science-and-religion/.

Priests for Equality. *The Inclusive Bible: The First Egalitarian Translation.* Lanham: Rowman & Littlefield, 2007.

ProgressiveChristianity.org. "The Core Values of Progressive Christianity," 2022. https://progressivechristianity.org/the-core-values-of-progressive-christianity/.

Sagan, Carl. *Cosmos.* New York: Ballentine Books, 1980.

"Toxic Wastes and Race in the United States: A National Report on the Racial and Socio-Economic Characteristics of Communities with Hazardous Waste Sites." United Church of Christ Commission for Racial Justice, 1987.